AA⌐

DEVOLVED ASSESSMENT KIT

Foundation Unit 4

Supplying Information for Management Control

In this June 2001 edition

This Devolved Assessment Kit follows the revised Foundation Standards of Competence. It contains:

- The **revised Standards in full**, including guidance from the AAT on **evidence requirements, sources of evidence and assessment strategy**

- **Practice activities** to bring you up to speed on certain areas of the Standards

- **Trial Run Devolved Assessments**

- AAT's **Sample Simulation** for this unit

All activities and assessments have full solutions included in this Kit.

FOR 2001 AND 2002 DEVOLVED ASSESSMENTS

BPP Publishing
June 2001

First edition August 2000

Second edition June 2001

ISBN 0 7517 6403 5 (Previous edition 07517 6233 4)

British Library Cataloguing-in-Publication Data
*A catalogue record for this book
is available from the British Library*

Published by

*BPP Publishing Limited
Aldine House, Aldine Place
London W12 8AW*

www.bpp.com

*Printed in Great Britain by W M Print
45-47 Frederick Street
Walsall
West Midlands
WS2 9NE*

We are grateful to the Lead Body for Accounting for permission to reproduce extracts from the Standards of Competence for Accounting.

CONTENTS

Page

	Activities	**Answers**
Practice activities	3	15

> Practice activities are short activities directly related to the actual content of the BPP Interactive Text. They are graded pre-assessment and assessment.

	Activities	**Answers**
Practice devolved assessments	23	45

> Practice devolved assessments consist of a number of tasks covering certain areas of the Standards of Competence but are not full assessments.

	Activities	**Answers**
Trial run devolved assessments	57	93

> Trial run devolved assessments are of similar scope to full simulations.

	Activities	**Answers**
AAT sample simulation	105	127

	Activities	**Answers**
Lecturers' resource pack activities	137	-

> Lecturers' resource pack activities are practice activities and assessments for lecturers to set in class or for homework. The answers are given in the BPP Lecturers' Resource Pack.

Contents

ORDER FORM

REVIEW FORM & FREE PRIZE DRAW

Activities Answers Done

PRACTICE ACTIVITIES

Chapter 1 Introduction to management information

		Activities	Answers	Done
1	Cost code	3	15	☐
2	Management accounts	3	15	☐

Chapter 2 Types of income and expenditure

3	Cost elements	4	15	☐
4	Cost classifications	4	15	☐
5	Prime cost	4	15	☐
6	Capital expenditure	4	15	☐
7	Depreciation	4	15	☐
8	Investment centre	4	16	☐

Chapter 3 Documentation of income and expenditure

9	Letter of enquiry	5	16	☐
10	Purchase order	5	16	☐
11	Credit note	5	16	☐
12	Deductions	5	16	☐
13	Documents	5	16	☐
14	Pan	5	17	☐

Chapter 4 Coding income and expenditure

15	Computerised accounting systems	7	17	☐
16	Understanding	7	17	☐
17	Corrie Ltd	7	17	☐

Chapter 5 Reporting management information

18	Letter	8	17	☐
19	E-mail	8	18	☐
20	Data users and subjects	8	18	☐
21	Types of communication	8	18	☐

Chapter 6 Making comparisons

22	Comparisons	9	18	☐
23	Variance reporting	9	18	☐
24	Exception reporting	9	18	☐
25	Stock records	9	18	☐
26	Fred plc	10	19	☐

Chapter 7 Using management information for decision making

27	Contribution	11	19	☐
28	Covering costs	11	19	☐
29	Profit	11	19	☐

BPP
PUBLISHING

HOW TO USE THIS DEVOLVED ASSESSMENT KIT

Aims of this Devolved Assessment Kit

To provide the knowledge and practice to help you succeed in the devolved assessment for Foundation Unit 4 *Supplying Information for Management Control.*

To pass the devolved assessment you need a thorough understanding in all areas covered by the standards of competence.

To tie in with the other components of the BPP Effective Study Package to ensure you have the best possible chance of success.

Interactive Text

This covers all you need to know for devolved assessment for Unit 4. Icons clearly mark key areas of the text. Numerous activities throughout the text help you practise what you have just learnt.

Devolved Assessment Kit

When you have understood and practised the material in the Interactive Text, you will have the knowledge and experience to tackle this Devolved Assessment Kit for Unit 4. This aims to get you through the devolved assessment, whether in the form of a simulation or workplace assessment. It contains the AAT's Sample Simulation for Unit 4 plus other Simulations.

Recommended approach to this Devolved Assessment Kit

(a) To achieve competence in all units you need to be able to do **everything** specified by the standards. Study the Interactive Text very carefully and do not skip any of it.

(b) Learning is an **active** process. Do **all** the activities as you work through the Interactive Text so you can be sure you really understand what you have read.

(c) After you have covered the material in the Interactive Text, work through this **Devolved Assessment Kit**.

(d) Try the **Practice Activities**. These are short activities, linked into the Standards of Competence, to reinforce your learning and consolidate the practice that you have had doing the activities in the Interactive Text.

(e) Then do the **Trial Run Devolved Assessments**. Although these are not yet fully at the level you can expect when you do a full devolved assessment, they do cover all the performance criteria of the elements indicated.

(f) Finally, try the AAT's **Sample Simulation** which gives you the clearest idea of what a full assessment will be like.

Remember this is a **practical** course.

(a) Try to relate the material to your experience in the workplace or any other work experience you may have had.

(b) Try to make as many links as you can to your study of the other units at this level.

Lecturers' resource pack activities

At the back of this Kit we have included a number of chapter-linked activities without answers to be attempted during classes. We have also included two practice devolved assessments without answers. The answers for this section are in the BPP Lecturers' Resource pack for this Unit.

BPP
PUBLISHING

UNIT 4 STANDARDS OF COMPETENCE

The structure of the Standards for Unit 4

The Unit commences with a statement of the **knowledge and understanding** which underpin competence in the Unit's elements.

The Unit of Competence is then divided into **elements of competence** describing activities which the individual should be able to perform.

Each element includes:

(a) A set of **performance criteria.** This defines what constitutes competent performance.

(b) A **range statement.** This defines the situations, contexts, methods etc in which competence should be displayed.

(c) **Evidence requirements.** These state that competence must be demonstrated consistently, over an appropriate time scale with evidence of performance being provided from the appropriate sources.

(d) **Sources of evidence.** These are suggestions of ways in which you can find evidence to demonstrate that competence. These fall under the headings: 'observed performance; work produced by the candidate; authenticated testimonies from relevant witnesses; personal account of competence; other sources of evidence.'

The elements of competence for Unit 4 *Supplying Information for Management Control* are set out below. Knowledge and understanding required for the unit as a whole are listed first, followed by the performance criteria and range statements for each element. Performance criteria are cross-referenced below to chapters in this Unit 4 *Supplying Information for Management Control* Interactive Text.

Unit 4: Supplying information for management control

What is the unit about?

This unit relates to the role of recognising and providing basic management information. This involves information relating to both costs and income and includes the comparison of actual costs and income against the previous period's data, the corresponding period's data and forecast data.

The first element involves recognising cost centres. It should be noted that in some organisations profit centres or investment centres will be used in place of cost centres, and these will differ depending on the organisation. The element also involves recognising elements of costs, coding income and expenditure and identifying and reporting obvious errors, such as the wrong code or excessive volumes. Individuals are required to extract information relating to the three elements of costs: materials, labour and expenses. The element, however, does not specifically relate to manufacturing as materials will include items such as consumables in service industries, and the majority of costs will probably be labour costs in those circumstances.

The second element is concerned with extracting information from a particular source, for example the previous period's data, and comparing that information with actual costs and income, in line with the organisational requirements. The individual is required to report discrepancies between the two in the appropriate format, ensuring confidentiality requirements are adhered to.

Knowledge and understanding

The business environment

- Types of cost centres, including profit centres and investment centres (Element 4.1)
- Costs, including wages, salaries, services and consumables (Element 4.1)

Accounting methods

- Identifying cost centres (Element 4.1)
- The purpose of management information: decision making; planning and control (Element 4.1)
- The make up of gross pay (Element 4.1)
- The relationship and integration of financial and management accounting (Element 4.1)
- Methods of presenting information (Element 4.2)
- Handling confidential information (Element 4.2)
- The role of management information in the organisation (Element 4.2)
- Awareness of the relationship between financial and management accounting (Element 4.2)

The organisation

- Relevant understanding of the organisation's accounting systems and administrative systems and procedures (Elements 4.1 and 4.2)
- The nature of the organisation's business transactions (Elements 4.1 and 4.2)
- The goods and services produced, bought and delivered by the organisation (Element 4.1)
- The cost centres within the organisation (Element 4.1)
- Organisational coding structures (Element 4.1)
- The organisation's confidentiality requirements (Element 4.2)
- House style for presentation of different types of documents (Element 4.2)

Element 4.1 Code and extract information

Performance criteria	Chapters in InteractiveText
1 Appropriate cost centres and elements of costs are recognised	1 - 4
2 Income and expenditure details are extracted from the relevant sources	2 - 4
3 Income and expenditure are coded correctly	4
4 Any problems in obtaining the necessary information are referred to the appropriate person	4
5 Errors are identified and reported to the appropriate person	4

Range statement

1 Elements of costs: materials; labour; expenses

2 Sources: purchase invoices; sales invoices; policy manual; payroll

3 Information: cost; income; expenditure

4 Errors: wrong codes; excessive volumes; wrong organisation

- Coding entries are located and established from organisational coding documentation

- Receipts and payments are analysed from range documents and amounts are coded to ledger accounts

- Witness testimony identifying coding as being correctly carried out. Personal statement

- Correspondence seeking further information to analyse cost to code. Witness testimony

- Correspondence/report employee identifying errors and source documents. Personal statement, job diary, critical incident report. Witness testimony

Element 4.2 Provide comparisons on costs and income

Performance criteria		Chapters in Interactive Text
1	Information requirements are clarified with the appropriate person	6 - 7
2	Information extracted from a particular source is compared with actual results	6 - 7
3	Discrepancies are identified	6 - 7
4	Comparisons are provided to the appropriate person in the required format	5 - 7
5	Organisational requirements for confidentiality are strictly followed	6

Range statement

1   Information: costs; income

2   Sources: previous period's data; corresponding period's data; forecast data; ledgers

3   Format: letter; memo; e-mail; note; report

4   Confidentiality requirements: sharing of information; storage of documents

- Correspondence checking information requirement. Witness testimony

- Standard cost report, budgetary control reports, management accounts, one-off report showing comparison data

- Correspondence reporting variances, differences, significant changes. Exception reports, job diary, critical incident report

- Correspondence across the range specified. Witness testimony

- Company policy on confidentiality, reports, and documents incorporating policy into practice. Witness testimony, personal statement

- **All the suggested workplace documents for this unit should be supplemented with other sources of evidence, such as personal statements, witness testimony and questioning. Assessors should ensure full coverage of the performance criteria, range and knowledge and understanding. The portfolio should contain a good mix of evidence using a variety of assessment methods.**

BPP PUBLISHING

ASSESSMENT STRATEGY

This Unit is assessed by **devolved assessment only**.

Devolved assessment

Devolved assessment is a means of collecting evidence of your ability to **carry out practical activities** and to **operate effectively in the conditions of the workplace** to the standards required. Evidence may be collected at your place of work, or at an Approved Assessment Centre by means of simulations of workplace activity, or by a combination of these methods.

If the Approved Assessment Centre is a **workplace**, you may be observed carrying out accounting activities as part of your normal work routine. You should collect documentary evidence of the work you have done, or contributed to, in an **accounting portfolio**. Evidence collected in a portfolio can be assessed in addition to observed performance or where it is not possible to assess by observation.

Where the Approved Assessment Centre is a **college or training organisation**, devolved assessment will be by means of a combination of the following.

(a) Documentary evidence of activities carried out at the workplace, collected by you in an **accounting portfolio**.

(b) Realistic **simulations** of workplace activities. These simulations may take the form of case studies and in-tray exercises and involve the use of primary documents and reference sources.

(c) **Projects and assignments** designed to assess the Standards of Competence.

If you are unable to provide workplace evidence you will be able to complete the assessment requirements by the alternative methods listed above.

Possible assessment methods

Where possible, evidence should be collected in the workplace, but this may not be a practical prospect for you. Equally, where workplace evidence can be gathered it may not cover all elements. The AAT regards performance evidence from simulations, case studies, projects and assignments as an acceptable substitute for performance at work, provided that they are based on the Standards and, as far as possible, on workplace practice.

There are a number of methods of assessing accounting competence. The list below is not exhaustive, nor is it prescriptive. Some methods have limited applicability, but others are capable of being expanded to provide challenging tests of competence.

Assessment method	Suitable for assessing
Performance of an accounting task either in the workplace or by simulation: eg preparing and processing documents, posting entries, making adjustments, balancing, calculating, analysing information etc by manual or computerised processes	**Basic task competence**. Adding supplementary oral questioning may help to draw out underpinning knowledge and understanding and highlight your ability to deal with contingencies and unexpected occurrences
General case studies. These are broader than simulations. They include more background information about the system and business environment	Ability to **analyse a system** and suggest ways of modifying it. It could take the form of a written report, with or without the addition of oral or written questions
Accounting problems/cases: eg a list of balances that require adjustments and the preparation of final accounts	Understanding of the **general principles of accounting** as applied to a particular case or topic
Preparation of flowcharts/diagrams. To illustrate an actual (or simulated) accounting procedure	**Understanding of the logic** behind a procedure, of controls, and of relationships between departments and procedures. Questions on the flow chart or diagram can provide evidence of underpinning knowledge and understanding
Interpretation of accounting information from an actual or simulated situation. The assessment could include non-financial information and written or oral questioning	**Interpretative competence**
Preparation of written reports on an actual or simulated situation	**Written communication skills**
Analysis of critical incidents, problems encountered, achievements	Your ability to handle **contingencies**
Listing of likely errors eg preparing a list of the main types of errors likely to occur in an actual or simulated procedure	Appreciation of the range of **contingencies** likely to be encountered. Oral or written questioning would be a useful supplement to the list
Outlining the organisation's policies, guidelines and regulations	Performance criteria relating to these aspects of competence. It also provides evidence of competence in **researching information**
Objective tests and short-answer questions	**Specific knowledge**
In-tray exercises	Your **task-management ability** as well as technical competence
Supervisors' reports	**General job competence**, personal effectiveness, reliability, accuracy, and time management. Reports need to be related specifically to the Standards of Competence

Assessment method	Suitable for assessing
Analysis of work logbooks/diaries	**Personal effectiveness**, time management etc. It may usefully be supplemented with oral questioning
Formal written answers to questions	**Knowledge and understanding** of the general accounting environment and its impact on particular units of competence
Oral questioning	**Knowledge and understanding** across the range of competence including organisational procedures, methods of dealing with unusual cases, contingencies and so on. It is often used in conjunction with other methods

PRACTICE ACTIVITIES

1 Introduction to management information

1 COST CODE   **Pre-assessment**

Define a cost code.

2 MANAGEMENT ACCOUNTS   **Pre-assessment**

The data used to prepare financial accounts and management accounts are the same. What are the main features of management accounts?

2   *Types of income and expenditure*

3   COST ELEMENTS   **Pre-assessment**

What are the three main elements of cost?

4   COST CLASSIFICATIONS   **Pre-assessment**

List four classifications of cost.

5   PRIME COST   **Pre-assessment**

Which elements of cost make up prime cost?

6   CAPITAL EXPENDITURE   **Pre-assessment**

What is capital expenditure?

7   DEPRECIATION   **Pre-assessment**

What is depreciation?

8   INVESTMENT CENTRE   **Pre-assessment**

What is an investment centre?

3 Documentation of income and expenditure

9   LETTER OF ENQUIRY   **Pre-assessment**

What is a letter of enquiry?

10   PURCHASE ORDER   **Pre-assessment**

Once a supplier has been selected, the buying department will prepare a purchase order in order to request that goods be supplied. Who are copies of the purchase order sent to?

11   CREDIT NOTE   **Pre-assessment**

When is a credit note usually issued?

12   DEDUCTIONS   **Pre-assessment**

List five deductions that might be made from employee's wages by an employer (both compulsory and authorised by employees).

13   DOCUMENTS   **Pre-assessment**

Which document(s) would you consult in order to check the following?

(a)   That goods sent to a customer have been received
(b)   Who authorised a purchase order
(c)   Total petty cash for the month
(d)   When goods which have been ordered will be delivered
(e)   Total Employer's National Insurance due for the month
(f)   That a price on a purchase invoice is as agreed
(g)   Who authorised a petty cash payment
(h)   The time spent on specific jobs by a factory worker
(i)   Whether purchased goods have been delivered
(j)   The coding of a sales invoice

14   PAN   **Assessment**

Janice Pan worked 42 hours for the administration department last week and she is paid at a rate of £10 per hour. Her normal working hours are 32 hours per week and overtime is paid at time and a quarter. Employer's NI is contributed at a rate of 12½% on earnings over £84 per week.

Complete the following payroll calculation sheet.

5

PAYROLL CALCULATION SCHEDULE		
NAME:		
DEPARTMENT:		
BASIC RATE:		
HOURS WORKED:		
HOURS FOR OVERTIME PREMIUM:		
	Calculation	**Amount** £
BASIC PAY		
OVERTIME PREMIUM		
EMPLOYER'S NIC		

4 Coding income and expenditure

15 COMPUTERISED ACCOUNTING SYSTESMS   Pre-assessment

What advantages do computerised accounting systems have over manual accounting systems?

16 UNDERSTANDING   Pre-assessment

Coding information correctly requires employees to have a good understanding of the organisation. In particular, what things do employees need to know?

17 CORRIE LTD   Assessment

Corrie Ltd has the following profit centres and codes.

310 – UK North
330 – UK Central
350 – UK South

The third digit denotes the type of sale

001 – Sale of Product A
002 – Sale of Product B
003 – Sale of Product C

Code the following:

(a)   Sale of Product B in Glasgow
(b)   Sale of Product A in London
(c)   Sale of Product C in Newcastle
(d)   Sale of Product B in Birmingham

BPP PUBLISHING

5 Reporting management information

18 LETTER

If you were to write a letter that started 'Dear Mr Smith' would you sign the letter

(a) Yours faithfully, or
(b) Yours sincerely.

19 E-MAIL

What advantages does E-mail have as a method of communication?

20 DATA USERS AND SUBJECTS

What are:

(a) Data users
(b) Data subjects?

21 TYPES OF COMMUNICATION

Do you think the following types of communication are suitable in the circumstances? If not, why not?

(a) A telephone call to check a coding query with another department.
(b) An E-mail to confirm a contract.
(c) A memorandum to report the results of a three-week investigation.
(d) A letter to request information from an overseas branch.
(e) A fax to send customer research findings to another division.

6 *Making comparisons*

22 COMPARISONS

Managers often make comparisons between actual data and other data. What are six of the most common financial comparisons?

23 VARIANCE REPORTING

What is variance reporting?

24 EXCEPTION REPORTING

What is exception reporting?

25 STOCK RECORDS

The computerised stock records of an off-license use a two-letter code to denote the type of drink, followed by one letter and two numbers to denote the make, followed by the bottle size in litres.

EXAMPLE: GIG12 0.75 is a 75 centilitre bottle of Gordon's gin.

The following whiskies are included in the stock report at the end of the accounting year.

Details	Size	Number
WHB15	0.70	14
WHF03	0.70	15
WHL03	0.75	5
WHM11	1.00	8
WHT09	0.75	23

A physical stock count finds the following.

14 × 0.70 bottles of Black and White (B15)
14 × 0.70 bottles of The Famous Grouse (F03)
5 × 0.70 bottles of Lagavulin (L03)
8 × 1.00 bottles of McLaren (M11)
22 × 0.75 bottles of Teachers (T09)

(a) Which stocks should be reported to management?
(b) Which stocks should be reported in the financial accounts?
(c) How might any discrepancies have arisen and how can you check them?

26 FRED PLC

You are the Accounts Assistant at Fred plc.

The following schedule is an example of the performance report which you produce every month for your boss, Margaret Barge the Management Accountant.

SALES PERFORMANCE REPORT – MAY 2001					
PERIOD	**MONTH**	**MONTH**	**YEAR TO DATE**	
PROFIT CENTRE	**ACTUAL £**	**BUDGET £**	**ACTUAL £**	**BUDGET £**
UNITED STATES				
UNITED KINGDOM				
EUROPE				
ASIA				

Task

What are the main uses of such a report?

ANSWERS TO CHAPTER 1: INTRODUCTION TO MANAGEMENT INFORMATION

1 COST CODE

A cost code is a 'shorthand' description of a cost using numbers, letters or a combination of both.

2 MANAGEMENT ACCOUNTS

Management accounts have the following features.

(a) They are used internally for use within a business only.

(b) They are recorded and presented in a way that is decided by management.

(c) They look at **past** data and also **future** data (for planning purposes).

(d) They are used to help management in **planning, control** and **decision making**.

ANSWERS TO CHAPTER 2: TYPES OF INCOME AND EXPENDITURE

3 COST ELEMENTS

The three main elements of cost are

- Materials
- Labour
- Expenses

4 COST CLASSIFICATIONS

Four categories of cost are

- Direct
- Indirect
- Variable
- Fixed

5 PRIME COST

Prime cost is made up of the following.

- Direct materials
- Direct labour
- Direct expenses

In other words, prime cost is the total direct costs.

6 CAPITAL EXPENDITURE

Capital expenditure is expenditure on long-term fixed assets which the business intends to retain for its own use.

7 DEPRECIATION

Depreciation is a cost which is associated with having fixed assets. Depreciation is the value of the asset which has been used up by the business in any given period.

8   INVESTMENT CENTRE

An investment centre is used where a manager is responsible for profit in relation to capital invested in his area.

ANSWERS TO CHAPTER 3: DOCUMENTATION OF INCOME AND EXPENDITURE

9   LETTER OF ENQUIRY

A letter of enquiry is a letter that is sent to suppliers in order to find out the following.

- Prices
- Delivery dates
- Charges
- Discounts available
- Terms of payment

10   PURCHASE ORDER

Copies of the purchase order are sent to the following.

- The supplier (to ask for the goods).
- The accounts department (for checking against the invoice when it arrives).
- The stores section (for updating the stock records).
- The goods received section (so they can expect the goods).

11   CREDIT NOTE

- When errors have been made on the suppliers sales invoice.
- If any goods received were damaged.
- If the invoice does not match the details on the delivery note.
- Output related pay

12   DEDUCTIONS

- Income tax (paid to the Inland Revenue)
- Employees' National Insurance (paid to the NI Contributions Agency)
- Employee pension contributions
- SAYE (Save As You Earn schemes)
- Subscriptions

13   DOCUMENTS

- (a) Signed delivery or consignment note
- (b) Purchase requisition
- (c) Petty cash record sheet
- (d) The advice note
- (e) The payroll
- (f) Purchase order
- (g) Petty cash slip
- (h) Job card or clock card
- (i) Goods received note
- (j) Coding list and/or policy manual

14   PAN

PAYROLL CALCULATION SCHEDULE		
NAME:	Janice Pan	
DEPARTMENT:	Administration	
BASIC RATE:	£10 per hour	
HOURS WORKED:	42	
HOURS FOR OVERTIME PREMIUM:	10	
	Calculation	**Amount** £
BASIC PAY	42 hrs × £10	420
OVERTIME PREMIUM	10 hrs × £10 × 0.25	25
EMPLOYER'S NIC	£420 + £25 = £425 £425 − £84 = £331 £331 × 12.5%	41.37

ANSWERS TO CHAPTER 4: CODING INCOME AND EXPENDITURE

15   COMPUTERISED ACCOUNTING SYSTEMS

(a) They record and retrieve information quickly and easily.
(b) They are automatically accurate and have built-in checking facilities.
(c) They can file a large amount of information in a small space.
(d) They are capable of sorting information in may different ways.

16   UNDERSTANDING

- The main activities of the organisation
- The main sources of income
- The main items of expenditure
- Details of the organisational structure

17   CORRIE LTD

(a) 312
(b) 351
(c) 313
(d) 332

ANSWERS TO CHAPTER 5: REPORTING MANAGEMENT INFORMATION

18   LETTER

'Yours sincerely' is used when writing to a named person. (Yours faithfully is used when writing to 'Dear Sir').

19   E-MAIL

E-mail has the following advantages.

- Speed
- Economy
- Efficiency
- Security

20   DATA USERS AND SUBJECTS

(a)   Data users are organisations or individuals which use personal data covered by the Act.

(b)   Data subjects are individuals on whom personal data is held.

21   TYPES OF COMMUNICATION

(a)   Yes, this is fine.

(b)   No. A contract confirmation will need a signature.

(c)   No. This level of detail almost certainly needs a formal report.

(d)   An e-mail would be quicker and cheaper if access were available.

(e)   This is fine if the information is not confidential.

ANSWERS TO CHAPTER 6: MAKING COMPARISONS

22   COMPARISONS

(a)   Comparisons with previous periods.

(b)   Comparisons with corresponding periods.

(c)   Comparisons with forecasts.

(d)   Comparisons with budgets.

(e)   Comparisons within organisations.

(f)   Comparisons with other organisations.

23   VARIANCE REPORTING

Variance reporting is the reporting of differences between budgeted and actual performance.

24   EXCEPTION REPORTING

Exception reporting is the reporting only of those variances which exceed a certain amount or percentage.

25   STOCK RECORDS

(a)   Comparing the physical count with the computer records reveals that both The Famous Grouse and Teachers are one bottle short of the recorded amount and the bottle size of Lagavulin is 0.70 instead of 0.75.

(b)   The physical count is likely to be more reliable than computerised records so this must be reported in the financial and management accounts (this will require accounting adjustments).

(c) The 'missing' bottles could be due to theft (by staff or shoplifters). The error on the bottle size could be due to keying in the original invoice incorrectly (check to see).

26 FRED PLC

- To show how sales performance is split between different profit centres

- To show sales values for each month and for the year-to-date

- To compare actual sales performance with budgeted sales performance

- To enable variances to be calculated

- To obtain explanations from managers whose profit centres are underperforming

ANSWERS TO CHAPTER 7: USING MANAGEMENT INFORMATION FOR DECISION MAKING

27 CONTRIBUTION

Each packet of tablets contributes £0.75 towards fixed costs (£1.50 – £0.75).

28 COVERING COSTS

$$\frac{£150,000}{£0.75} = 200,000$$

29 PROFIT

$(500,000 \times £0.75) - £150,000$

$= £375,000 - £150,000$

$= £225,000$

PRACTICE DEVOLVED ASSESSMENTS

Practice devolved assessment 1: Sectex plc

Performance criteria

The following performance criteria are covered in this practice devolved assessment

Element 4.2 Provide comparisons on costs and income

(i)   Information requirements are clarified with the appropriate person

(v)   Organisational requirements for confidentiality are strictly followed

Note

This practice devolved assessment asks you to convey confidentiality requirements to a third party and to clarify exactly what the third party requires.

SECTEX PLC

Sectex plc develops and sells computer software. One day the Finance Director receives the following letter from a local college.

Bankdown College of Technology
Darting Road
Eastdown
Hants SO22 9BZ

Telephone 0193 65407

4 March 2001

Our ref BT/js

The Finance Director
Sectex plc
Bournemouth Road
Southampton SO17 9BJ

Dear Sir,

Re: student work experience

We have three students on our Business Finance course who are particularly interested in the information technology industry. I am therefore writing to ask you if you would consider offering one or more of them a two-month work placement this summer. They are all computer literate and have knowledge of basic accounting.

If you are able to help them with work this summer, the placement would be at no cost to your company and the experience would be immensely valuable to the students in both general terms and the dissertations they are working on. Their topics are all based on the UK software industry and cover the following.

Susan Wells   Pricing and competition
Jason Bing   Research and development costs
Barry Mann   Marketing strategies

I do hope that you can help us in this important aspect of educating these young people and look forward to receiving your reply.

Yours faithfully,

B Turner
(Brian Turner: Head of Business Studies)

Task

In this competitive industry, Sectex plc's company policy is to maintain strict confidentiality on its costs, pricing and marketing strategies. The Finance Director asks you to draft a reply to the college pointing out the company's policy on confidentiality and to ask if the students are still interested in a placement over the summer.

Practice devolved assessment 2: Salix plc

Performance criteria

The following performance criteria are covered in this practice devolved assessment

Element 4.1 Code and extract information

(iv)   Any problems in obtaining the necessary information are referred to the appropriate person

Element 4.2 Provide comparisons on costs and income

(i)   Information requirements are clarified with the appropriate person

(v)   Organisational requirements for confidentiality are strictly followed

Note

This practice devolved assessment requires you to respond to a situation where a request for information conflicts with the rules of the organisation.

BPP PUBLISHING

SALIX PLC

Salix plc is a multinational company that makes and sells pharmaceutical products all over the world. It provides very detailed analyses of sales (in units and £) by country and by product for internal use, but only publishes the minimum information required by company law and accounting standards as such information could be useful to competitors. Some of the ingredients used are tested on animals but, again, such information is only revealed as and when required by law. All employees have to sign a confidentiality agreement when they join the company confirming that they will follow the company manual and will not talk to the press.

There has been some pressure from shareholders for the company to publish an 'Ethical and Environmental Report' for issue with the financial accounts and the company has hired external consultants to advise them on whether they should do this. When they start work the consultants ask you for copies of the following.

- All sales analyses produced in the last six months
- A list of products tested on animals
- Details of the testings undertaken

You consult the confidentiality section of the company policy manual, which begins as follows. 'Most company information should not be released without written authority. When seeking authority, the use to which the information will be put must be clearly stated in writing by the user.

(a) No unpublished information on sales, prices or customers should be released from the sales department without authority from the sales manager.

(b) No information on suppliers should be released from the purchasing department without authority from the chief purchasing officer.

(c) Information on animal testing of products and ingredients is particularly sensitive and is held within the Research and Development Department. It will only be released to externals on the authority of a director.'

Task

How should you deal with the consultants' requests?

Practice devolved assessment 3: Local authority

Performance criteria

The following performance criteria are covered in this practice devolved assessment

Element 4.1 Code and extract information

(i)   Appropriate cost centres and elements of costs are recognised

Element 4.2 Provide comparisons on costs and income

(i)   Information requirements are clarified with the appropriate person

(iv)   Comparisons are provided to the appropriate person in the required format

Note

This practice devolved assessment asks you to compare the costs of providing a service using two different methods. You will need to decide which costs are relevant and use your common sense to think about the practicalities of both methods.

LOCAL AUTHORITY

You work for a local authority which is considering whether to outsource (ie use an external provider) its day-care services for elderly and disabled people in the local area. An external agency has quoted a fee of £9 per hour for providing the service using the authority's present accommodation. An internal report shows the costs of providing the current service.

	£ per hour
Gross labour cost for attendants	7.00
Supervision costs	1.50
Accommodation costs	2.00
Central administration costs	2.50
Total cost	13.00

Tasks

(a)   What saving (if any) per hour would the local authority make if it accepted the external agency's quote? What other factors, apart from cost savings, should be taken into account?

(b)   Write a note for attachment to the cost report which explains the savings possible if the local authority decides to outsource its day-care services. Identify any other information that should be considered when making the decision.

Practice devolved assessment 4: Linus Ltd

Performance criteria

The following performance criteria are covered in this practice devolved assessment

Element 4.2 Provide comparisons on costs and income

(v) Organisational requirements for confidentiality are strictly followed

Note

This practice devolved assessment asks you to consider which general confidentiality requirements are not being met by Linus Ltd (without referring to a written company policy).

LINUS LTD

The personnel manager of Linus Ltd has decided to carry out a 'confidentiality and security' audit of employee records and has asked you to investigate how well they are protected. Your findings are shown below.

(a) There is a paper file for each employee giving details of their age, sex, employment, pay rate, sickness details and so on. These files are held in a lockable cupboard in the personnel department which is unlocked by the supervisor each morning and locked when she goes home. Anyone working on a file takes it from the cupboard and keeps it on their desk until they have finished with it. Not all the desks in the department have locks.

(b) Details of pay, tax codes, sick pay and so on are held on the computerised payroll system which is accessed by password only. Three people have access to this password and one of them has written it on a post-it note stuck to his computer.

(c) One employee is intending to sue the company for work-related repetitive strain injury and has been refused permission to check the sickness records on her personnel file.

(d) A college student, gaining work experience in the company for the summer, is producing an equal opportunities report for his college looking at employee records to investigate the gender, age and race proportions at various levels of seniority in the company. No permission has been sought from the employees.

Task

Write a short, informal, preliminary report to the personnel manager pointing out any potential problems with confidentiality and/or security and suggesting any possible improvements.

Practice devolved assessment 5: Herefordshire Juices Ltd

Performance criteria

The following performance criteria are covered in this practice devolved assessment

Element 4.1 Code and extract information

(i)   Appropriate cost centres and elements of cost are recognised

(ii)   Income and expenditure details are extracted from the relevant sources

(iii)   Income and expenditure are coded properly

Note

This practice devolved assessment requires you to code sales and purchases invoices and to complete a coding extract for income and expenditure. It also requires you to establish income and expenditure balances at 31 July 2001 using the completed extract for income and expenditure.

HEREFORDSHIRE JUICES LTD

You work as an accounting technician in the administration department of Herefordshire Juices Ltd, a producer of organic juices.

Your main tasks are the coding of income and expenditure from all source documents.

Profit centres

Herefordshire Juices Ltd makes four types of juice which are sold in the following areas of Britain only.

Profit centre code

•	England - north	100
•	England – south	200
•	Scotland	300
•	Wales	400

The third digit denotes the type of juice sold.

•	Organic apple juice	= 1
•	Organic orange juice	= 2
•	Organic tomato juice	= 3
•	Organic elderflower juice	= 4

Cost centres

Production cost centres are coded as follows.

600	Cutting
610	Pressing
620	Filtering
630	Bottling
640	Administration
650	Stores
660	Marketing and distribution

The third digit denotes the type of expenditure.

•	Material	= 1
•	Labour	= 2
•	Expenses	= 3

Tasks

(a) Code the sales and purchases invoices shown below and complete the coding extract for income and expenditure on page 37. For each relevant code you should post the amendment and update the balance. Ignore VAT (this is coded automatically on receipt of the invoice).

(b) Update the list of ledger balances for the month of July 2001 by posting the amended coding extract that you completed in task (a) above to the income and expenditure extract on page 38.

Herefordshire Juices Ltd

Mill Stream Industrial Estate
Faircombe
Herefordshire HR8 2AZ

VAT NO: 27272626X
TEL NO: 05 4438844
FAX NO: 054438845

TAX POINT: 30 July 2001

SALES INVOICE

To:
Stones Organic Foods
Manchester Industrial Estate
Manchester MN22 5AS

INVOICE NO: 222

Details	No	Net £	Total £
1 litre organic apple juice	500	0.85	425.00
1 litre organic orange juice	500	0.95	475.00
TOTAL BEFORE VAT			900.00
VAT			157.50
TOTAL INCLUDING VAT			1,057.50

Herefordshire Juices Ltd

Mill Stream Industrial Estate
Faircombe
Herefordshire HR8 2AZ

VAT NO: 27272626X
TEL NO: 05 4438844
FAX NO: 054438845

TAX POINT: 30 July 2001

SALES INVOICE

To:
Home Counties Organic Foods
Wriggley Industrial Estate
Holden-on-Thames
Surrey TN14 7AN

INVOICE NO: 223

Details	No	Net	Total
		£	£
1 litre organic tomato juice	300	1.00	300.00
1 litre organic elderflower juice	250	1.10	275.00
TOTAL BEFORE VAT			575.00
VAT			100.63
TOTAL INCLUDING VAT			675.63

Glass and Filters plc

Juniper Industrial Estate
Elderflower Way
Slaptonnery
Devon DR1 7AP

Invoice No: 6633

VAT NO: 246 346 446
TEL NO: 01111-22222
FAX NO: 01111-22223

TAX POINT: 29/07/00

INVOICE TO:

Herefordshire Juices Ltd
Mill Stream Industrial Estate
Faircombe
Herefordshire HR8 2AZ

	£
1,000 1 litre bottles @ £0.06 per bottle to be delivered to your bottling department	60.00
100 Juice filters @ £25 each to be delivered to your filtering department	2,500.00
TOTAL BEFORE VAT	2,560.00
VAT	448.00
TOTAL INCLUDING VAT	3,008.00

BPP PUBLISHING

Staff Galore Ltd

The High Street
Faircombe
Herefordshire HR8 2AY

INVOICE NO: 12345

VAT NO: 123 456 789
TAX POINT: 27/-7/01

TEL NO: 1234 56788
FAX NO: 1234 56789

INVOICE TO:

Herefordshire Juices Ltd
Mill Stream Industrial Estate
Faircombe
Herefordshire HR8 2AZ

Provision of temporary staff for your
stores department

10 days @ £135 per day   £1,350

CODING EXTRACT – INCOME AND EXPENDITURE – JULY 2001
(ROUNDED TO NEAREST £)

Code	Balance £	Amendment £	Updated balance £
101	3,891		
102	2,741		
103	3,347		
104	4,245		
201	2,937		
202	2,429		
203	3,846		
204	3,476		
301	3,731		
302	4,169		
303	5,231		
304	4,576		
401	4,741		
402	1,146		
403	2,043		
404	4,376		
621	907		
622	364		
631	416		
632	769		
641	661		
642	700		
651	674		
652	453		

EXTRACT INCOME AND EXPENDITURE BALANCES – Y/E 30.9.01			
Ledger account	*Balance at 30/06/2001*	*Amount coded July 2001*	*Balance at 31/07/2001*
	£	£	£
Sales			
Organic apple juice			
- England North	36,914		
- England South	25,921		
- Scotland	33,579		
- Wales	42,999		
Organic orange juice			
- England North	28,110		
- England South	24,861		
- Scotland	36,521		
- Wales	10,333		
Organic tomato juice			
- England North	30,382		
- England South	34,417		
- Scotland	46,970		
- Wales	16,873		
Organic elderflower juice			
- England North	40,680		
- England South	34,821		
- Scotland	44,118		
- Wales	38,394		
Expenditure			
Filtering			
- Materials	20,663		
- Labour	3,276		
Bottling			
- Materials	4,284		
- Labour	6,291		
Administration			
- Materials	6,951		
- Labour	7,241		
Stores			
- Materials	6,721		
- Labour	17,225		

Practice devolved assessment 6: Kingfisher plc

Performance criteria

The following performance criteria are covered in this practice devolved assessment

Element 4.2 Provide comparisons on costs and income

(ii)   Information extracted from a particular source is compared with actual results

(iii) Discrepancies are identified

(iv) Comparisons are provided to the appropriate person in the required format

Note

This practice devolved assessment requires you to complete a performance report for the total costs of production cost centres of an organisation. It also requires you to complete a variance report and to report on any variances which are more than 10% from budget and to complete a sales performance report which compares actual results with a budgeted results.

BPP PUBLISHING

KINGFISHER PLC

You work as an accounting technician in the accounts department of Kingfisher plc, a producer of maps in England. Kingfisher plc has a year end 31 December 2001. Kingfisher plc makes road maps, street maps and city maps which are sold via the following outlets.

- Postal order forms
- Bookshops
- Internet
- Petrol stations

The following schedule showing income and expenditure balances was prepared at 31.8.2001

Ledger account	August 2001 expenditure £	Balance at 31.8.2001 £
Sales		
Road maps		
- Postal order forms	19,458	142,141
- Bookshops	21,228	120,462
- Internet	20,031	136,023
- Petrol stations	20,847	169,820
Street maps		
- Postal order forms	13,707	136,996
- Bookshops	15,538	173,777
- Internet	17,381	166,229
- Petrol stations	26,108	226,111
City maps		
- Postal order forms	16,738	115,970
- Bookshops	14,047	114,996
- Internet	20,157	143,602
- Petrol stations	22,881	172,546
Expenditure		
Printing		
- Material	24,081	61,476
- Labour	5,734	36,679
- Expenses	10,220	56,803
Wrapping		
- Material	4,108	33,455
- Labour	2,458	18,310
- Expenses	5,287	22,523
Packing		
- Material	1,821	21,105
- Labour	2,254	20,707
- Expenses	3,892	28,375

Tasks

(a)   Your boss, Mr Mapp has asked you to complete the performance report for total costs of the production cost centres (printing, wrapping and packing) shown below for the month of August and the year to 31.8.01

(b)   Complete the discrepancy (variance) report shown below and report on any variance which is more than 10% from budget for the month of August and the year to 31.8.01.

(c)   Complete the sales performance report for total sales shown on page 42 for the month of August and the year to 31 August 2001.

KINGFISHER PLC
PERFORMANCE REPORT
PRODUCTION COST CENTRES
TOTAL COSTS – AUGUST 2001

	Month – August 2001		Year to date	
	Actual £	Budget £	Actual £	Budget £
MATERIAL		36,167		113,900
LABOUR		10,750		66,167
EXPENSES		16,250		92,365

KINGFISHER PLC
DISCREPANCY (VARIANCE) REPORT
PRODUCTION COST CENTRES
AUGUST 2001

COST / PERIOD	MONTH £	YEAR TO DATE £
MATERIAL		
LABOUR		
EXPENSES		
COMMENT		

BPP PUBLISHING

PROFIT CENTRE \ PERIOD	MONTH ACTUAL £	MONTH BUDGET £	YEAR TO DATE ACTUAL £	YEAR TO DATE BUDGET £
POSTAL ORDER FORMS		49,000		392,500
BOOKSHOPS		54,500		416,250
INTERNET		56,400		443,200
PETROL STATIONS		71,050		582,300

Table title:

KINGFISHER PLC
SALES PERFORMANCE REPORT
AUGUST 2001

Answers to practice devolved assessments

1   **SECTEX PLC**

Your letter might look something like this.

SECTEX PLC

Bournemouth Road
Southampton SO17 9BJ

Telephone 0193 79450

7 March 2001

Mr Brian Turner
Head of Business Studies
Bankdown College of Technology
Darting Road
Eastdown
Hants SO22 9BZ

Your ref: BT/js

Dear Mr Turner,

Re: Student work placements

Thank you for your letter dated March 4th. As a company we are keen to do all that we can in order to help local organisations and, in principle, we should like to provide work experience for your students. We are, however, very concerned that information relating to the prices, costs, marketing strategies of Sectex plc remain strictly confidential. I am sure you will understand the necessity for this in an industry as competitive as ours.

We may be prepared to offer your students experience of accounting work but would have to be assured of their absolute discretion regarding our company's confidential information. They could not, for example, use any of our company details in their dissertations. If you think they will still be interested with these restrictions in force, please telephone me to discuss the matter further.

Yours sincerely,

J Perkins

---

2   **SALIX PLC**

It is clear that the information required by the consultants falls within the rules of confidentiality so you should not release it but you can give them advice on how to obtain permission for its release. This can probably best be dealt with verbally but you will need to explain the following points.

(a)   You are not allowed to release the information because this would go against company policy and the confidentiality agreement that you have signed.

(b)   Any requests to release confidential information:

    (i)   Must come from them (as the users)
    (ii)   Must be in writing
    (iii)   Must include an explanation of how the information will be used

(c) Sales analyses may only be released with the authority of the sales manager. Animal testing information, although held in the Research and Development Department, can only be released with the authority of a director.

3   LOCAL AUTHORITY

(a) (i)   Attendants' labour costs would be saved but these are less than the £9 quoted.

(ii)   Supervision costs may be saved if the agency provides adequate supervision within the quoted price. This still only totals £8.50 (£7.00 + £1.50).

(iii) If the same accommodation is used, then accommodation costs will still be incurred. You will need to investigate whether these costs will remain the same.

Central administration costs probably represent a share of the local authority's total administration costs but you do not know the basis on which they have been shared out. It is unlikely that outsourcing this service will affect the total costs significantly and there will also be a cost associated with accepting the contract. It cannot be assumed that £2.50 will be saved.

Other factors to consider include what will happen to the existing service staff if the quote is accepted and what contracts of employment will they have? Will redundancy payments have to be made? In the longer term, what guarantees are there about future price rises? What will happen if the agency's performance is below standard?

(b) The note could look something like this

DAY-CARE SERVICES – OUTSOURCED AND IN-HOUSE

The attached cost report shows the costs currently allocated to the day-care service. An external agency has quoted a figure of £9 per hour to provide the services but further information will be required in order to carry out a full evaluation.

(a) Are supervision costs included in this price and if so, will the level of supervision be adequate?

(b) Will accommodation costs remain the same?

(c) What administration costs will be incurred in carrying out the administration of the contract and the monitoring of performance?

(d) Will the authority incur any other costs, eg redundancy payments?

If adequate supervision is included in the £9 and accommodation costs remain unchanged, then possible savings will depend on the administration costs incurred as a result of running the contract. If these administration costs amount to less than £0.50 per hour, savings will not be made by outsourcing day-care services to an external agency.

---

4   LINUS LTD

SECURITY OF PERSONNEL RECORDS
PRELIMINARY REPORT

To...............................
By...............................
Dated...........................

Having inspected the personnel department, I have identified the following problems.

(a)   Paper personnel records are held in a cupboard with open access during the day, although it is locked overnight. Files being processed are left on desks and not all desks can be locked.

(b)   The computerised payroll system is password protected but the password is not kept secure. It is on open display at one workstation.

(c)   One employee has been refused access to her own personnel record.

(d)   The equal opportunities report being produced by a college student involves processing sensitive data about employees. It appears that permission has not been obtained from the employees concerned.

I suggest the following actions could improve security and confidentiality.

(a)   The cupboard containing employee files should be locked at all times and any files required should be signed out to a specific member of staff.

(b)   Files should be returned and signed back in every evening.

(c)   Anyone working on a file who leaves their desk should lock the file away, in their desk (if possible) or in the cupboard (if not possible).

(d)   The payroll password should be changed and those using it should be reminded that it is confidential.

(e)   Staff should be reminded that employees have the right to inspect their own personnel files.

(f)   The equal opportunities report requires permission from employees. If this is not possible, the report should be abandoned.

BPP PUBLISHING

5   HEREFORDSHIRE LTD

(a)

CODING EXTRACT – INCOME AND EXPENDITURE – JULY 2001 (ROUNDED TO NEAREST £)			
Code	Balance £	Amendment £	Updated balance £
101	3,891	425	4,316
102	2,741	475	3,216
103	3,347		3,347
104	4,245		4,245
201	2,937		2,937
202	2,429		2,429
203	3,846	300	4,146
204	3,476	275	3,751
301	3,731		3,731
302	4,169		4,169
303	5,231		5,231
304	4,576		4,576
401	4,741		4,741
402	1,146		1,146
403	2,043		2,043
404	4,376		4,376
621	907	2,500	3,407
622	364		364
631	416	60	476
632	769		769
641	661		661
642	700		700
651	674		674
652	453	1,350	1,803

(b)

EXTRACT INCOME AND EXPENDITURE BALANCES – Y/E 30.9.01			
Ledger account	*Balance at 30/06/2001*	*Amount coded July 2001*	*Balance at 31/07/2001*
	£	£	£
Sales			
Organic apple juice			
- England North	36,914	4,316	41,230
- England South	25,921	2,937	28,858
- Scotland	33,579	3,731	37,310
- Wales	42,999	4,741	47,740
Organic orange juice			
- England North	28,110	3,216	31,326
- England South	24,861	2,429	27,290
- Scotland	36,521	4,169	40,690
- Wales	10,333	1,146	11,479
Organic tomato juice			
- England North	30,382	3,347	33,729
- England South	34,417	4,146	38,563
- Scotland	46,970	5,231	52,201
- Wales	16,873	2,043	18,916
Organic elderflower juice			
- England North	40,680	4,245	44,925
- England South	34,821	3,751	38,572
- Scotland	44,118	4,576	48,694
- Wales	38,394	4,376	42,770
Expenditure			
Filtering			
- Materials	20,663	3,407	24,070
- Labour	3,276	364	3,640
Bottling			
- Materials	4,284	476	4,760
- Labour	6,291	769	7,060
Administration			
- Materials	6,951	661	7,612
- Labour	7,241	700	7,941
Stores			
- Materials	6,721	674	7,395
- Labour	17,225	1,803	19,028

BPP PUBLISHING

6 KINGFISHER PLC

(a)

KINGFISHER PLC PERFORMANCE REPORT PRODUCTION COST CENTRES TOTAL COSTS – AUGUST 2001				
	Month – August 2001		*Year to date*	
	Actual £	*Budget* £	*Actual* £	*Budget* £
MATERIAL	30,010	36,167 ·	116,036	113,900
LABOUR	10,446	10,750	75,696	66,167
EXPENSES	19,399	16,250	107,701	92,365

Workings

	Printing £	*Wrapping* £	*Packing* £	*Total* £
August 2000				
Material	24,081	4,108	1,821	30,010
Labour	5,734	2,458	2,254	10,446
Expenses	10,220	5,287	3,892	19,399
Year to date				
Material	61,476	33,455	21,105	116,036
Labour	36,679	18,310	20,707	75,696
Expenses	56,803	22,523	28,375	107,701

(b)

KINGFISHER PLC DISCREPANCY (VARIANCE) REPORT PRODUCTION COST CENTRES AUGUST 2001		
PERIOD / COST	MONTH £	YEAR TO DATE £
MATERIAL	£6,157 (F)	£2,136 (A)
LABOUR	£304 (F)	£9,529 (A)
EXPENSES	£3,149 (A)	£15,336 (A)

COMMENT

The significant variances which are more than 10% from budget are:

Month variances
- Material = £6,157 (F) = 17%
- Expenses = £3,149 (A) = 19.4%

Year to date variances
- Labour = £9,529 (A) = 14.4%
- Expenses = £15,336 (A) = 16.6%

(c)

KINGFISHER PLC SALES PERFORMANCE REPORT AUGUST 2001				
PERIOD / PROFIT CENTRE	MONTH ACTUAL £	MONTH BUDGET £	YEAR TO DATE ACTUAL £	YEAR TO DATE BUDGET £
POSTAL ORDER FORMS	49,903	49,000	395,107	392,500
BOOKSHOPS	50,813	54,500	409,235	416,250
INTERNET	57,569	56,400	445,854	443,200
PETROL STATIONS	69,836	71,050	568,477	582,300

Workings

	Road maps £	Street maps £	City maps £	Total £
Month actual				
Postal order forms	19,458	13,707	16,738	49,903
Bookshops	21,228	15,538	14,047	50,813
Internet	20,031	17,381	20,157	57,569
Petrol stations	20,847	26,108	22,881	69,836
Year to date actual				
Postal order forms	142,141	136,996	115,970	395,107
Bookshops	120,462	173,777	114,996	409,235
Internet	136,023	166,229	143,602	445,854
Petrol stations	169,820	226,111	172,546	568,477

TRIAL RUN DEVOLVED ASSESSMENTS

Trial run devolved assessment 1: Pyropraktek Ltd

Trial run devolved assessment 1: Pyropraktek Ltd

Performance criteria

The following performance criteria are covered in this trial run devolved assessment

Element 4.1 Code and extract information

(i)   Appropriate cost centres and elements of cost are recognised

(ii)   Income and expenditure details are extracted from the relevant sources

(iii)   Income and expenditure are coded correctly

(iv)   Any problems in obtaining the necessary information are referred to the appropriate person

(v)   Errors are identified and reported to the appropriate person

Element 4.2 Provide comparisons on costs and income

(i)   Information requirements are clarified with the appropriate person

(ii)   Information extracted from a particular source is compared with actual results

(iii)   Discrepancies are identified

(iv)   Comparisons are provided to the appropriate person in the required format

(v)   Organisation requirements for confidentiality are strictly followed

Notes on completing this trial run devolved assessment.

This assessment is designed to test your ability to code and check financial data taken from sales invoices, purchase invoices and payroll records.

You are provided with all the necessary information and data to perform the specified tasks.

You are allowed 3 hours to complete your work

Please check your work carefully as complete accuracy is required.

You should work in black ink or biro – NOT in pencil. Errors should be crossed out neatly and clearly

THE SITUATION

You are employed in the accounts department of Pyropraktek Ltd, a company manufacturing flares and fireworks. Pyropraktek Ltd is split into four divisions:

- 'Military and Marine', usually called M&M
- 'Exhibition and Retail', known as E&R
- Design and Development (D&D)
- Administration and Services (A&S)

The M&M division produces distress flares for yachts and ships which are sold to shipping companies and chandlers, plus heat-seeking missile decoys for military aircraft which are sold to the UK Ministry of Defence or to foreign governments. E&R make boxed fireworks for sale to the general public via retailers, specialised fireworks for public displays which are sold direct to the user, warning rockets and maroons.

Each of Pyropraktek Ltd's divisions is an investment centre.

(a)   The M&M division has two profit centres: UK Sales and Overseas Sales.

(b)   The E&R division has three profit centres: Direct Sales (for display fireworks sales), Retailer Sales (for boxed fireworks sales) and Internal Sales.

The Internal Sales profit centre is needed because the M&M sales team deals with all military and marine customers, and all overseas sales. As military and marine customers purchase all the warning rockets and maroons manufactured by the E&R division, the E&R division 'sells' them to the M&M division. Warning rockets, maroons and any E&R products sold overseas are transferred to M&M at variable cost plus 50%.

M&M and E&R are located at opposite sides of the airfield (East and West) to minimise the consequences of an accident. The administration offices, security department, maintenance department and canteen are located on the south side while the Design and Development buildings are on the northern edge of the airfield.

Pyropraktek's M&M and E&R divisions and the security department work three eight-hour shifts per day for seven days a week. Overtime is not permitted, except for maintenance staff who may work overnight and at weekends if necessary. It is company policy that all other staff in the D&D and A&S divisions should only work between 8.00 am and 6.00 pm from Monday to Friday.

Direct materials and packaging materials are delivered and coded straight to the production and packaging departments.

The investment, profit and cost centres, their codes and managers are listed below.

Pyropraktek Ltd – Extracts from account code list:

	Code	Code	Code	Manager
Investment centres:				
Military & Marine (M&M)	1			Joan Degas
Exhibition & Retail (E&R)	2			Alexander Surtees
Administration & Services (A&S)	3			Miriam Tek
Design & Development (D&D)	4			Maurice Tan
Profit centres:				
M&M - UK sales		10		Chris Jones
M&M - Overseas sales		11		Leslie Edge
E&R - Direct sales		20		Patrick Connolly
E&R - Retailer sales		21		Naomi Bloom
E&R - Internal sales		22		Alexander Surtees
Cost centre codes:				
Flares production department		13		Steve O'Connell
Decoys production department		14		Geraldine Maney
M&M packaging department		15		Cythia Rose
E&R production department		23		Ledward Bayley
E&R packaging department		24		Carlyle Duggan
Company Secretary		30		Miriam Tek
Maintenance department		31		Bob Smiley
Accounts department		32		Mina Nathwani
Security department		33		Sandra Henman
Fire department		34		Sandra Henman
Canteen		35		Jon Luciano
Personnel and training department		36		George Zemenides
Payroll department		37		Brenda Magumbe
Design department		40		Maurice Tan
Development department		41		Michelle Simpson
Account codes:				
Sales				
UK sales			1001	
Overseas sales			1002	
Internal sales			1011	
Materials				
Direct materials			2001	
Packaging materials			2002	
Internal purchases			2011	
Indirect materials			2021	
Employment costs:				
Direct wages			3001	
Indirect wages			3011	
Salaries			3012	
Employers' national insurance			3021	
Employers' pension contributions			3022	
Employers' liability insurance			3101	
Other employment costs			3102	
Distribution costs				
Air freight			4001	
Rail freight			4002	
Freight insurance			4003	
Other distribution costs			4004	
Expenses:				
Building insurance			5001	
Cleaning			5002	
Business rates			5003	
Bought in maintenance			5004	
Inspection charges			5005	
Electricity			5006	

BPP PUBLISHING

	Code	Code	Code	Manager
Telephone			5011	
Stationery			5012	
Vehicle rental & leasing charges			5021	
Vehicle running costs			5022	
Advertising			5031	
Third party insurance			5041	

Pyropraktek Ltd uses a seven figure accounts coding structure. An M&M UK sales invoice would be coded as follows:

Investment centre	Profit or cost centre		Account code			
1	1	0	1	0	0	1

You are responsible for coding purchase invoices and for checking the coding of sales invoices and payroll entries contained in Pyropraktek Ltd's accounting system.

THE TASKS TO BE COMPLETED

1   Examine the sales invoices list for the week ending 17 June 2001 on page 62.

(a)   Check that the codes are correct.

(b)   Note any invoices which you think have been coded incorrectly.

(c)   Enter all the details of any incorrectly coded invoices, including the CORRECT code, on the **sales invoices corrections** sheet on page 64.

2   Using the sales invoices list for the week ending 17 June 2001 on page 62.

(a)   Check through the listing for any peculiarities or discrepancies which you feel should be queried.

(b)   Inform the appropriate manager(s) of any inconsistencies found and seek clarification and/or instructions. Use the blank memo on page 65.

3   Study the purchase invoices on pages 66 to 71 and enter the appropriate seven figure account code below the purchase invoice serial number.

4   All A&S costs are apportioned to individual profit or cost centres using a variety of bases. Employers' liability insurance is apportioned by using each profit or cost centre's wages and salaries in the most recent month as a proportion of the total company figure for that month.

(a)   Contact the appropriate manager and request the figures that you need to apportion the employers' liability premium for 2001/2002 to profit and cost centres. Use the blank memo on page 72.

(b)   In your communication suggest ways in which you could receive the data to avoid any danger of disclosing private information.

5   Study the extract from Pyropraktek Ltd's payroll system on page 63.

(a)   Total the hours and gross pay for fire fighters and for security guards.
(b)   Enter these figures on the payroll posting slip on page 73.
(c)   Note any queries you may have in the notes column.

6   The accounting system produces weekly performance reports for each profit centre which compare actual results with the rolling budget. You check these performance reports before they are distributed to divisional managers and profit centre managers.

In Pyropraktek Ltd's rolling budget system the budget for the following twelve months is revised every three months. The most recent revision was carried out in April 2001. Customers' orders for all Pyropraktek Ltd's sales are placed several weeks in advance, so the actual out-turn for May 2001 should correspond closely with the budget.

(a)   Scrutinise the performance reports on page 63.

(b)   Note any significant differences from budget, using the blank memo on page 74.

DATA

Pyropraktek Ltd – Sales invoice list - w/e 17 June 2001						
Invoice no.	Date	Customer account no.	UK post code; Country; 9 = internal sales	Product	Account code	£
1371	12/06/01	BEN239	HA3 1SL	Display fireworks	2-20-1001	1,768.00
1372	12/06/01	MOD002	PO9 3QR	Flares	1-10-1001	32,587.50
1373	12/06/01	MOT024	Yemen	Decoys	1-11-1002	17,350.00
1374	12/06/01	MAM001	9	Warning rockets	2-21-1011	982.50
1375	13/06/01	KEN567	NW1 4QH	Display fireworks	1-20-1001	1,370.00
1376	13/06/01	HAR298	SP1 3UA	Boxed fireworks	2-21-1001	1,690.75
1377	13/06/01	PID661	India	Maroons	1-21-1002	1,302.90
1378	13/06/01	PID661	India	Warning rockets	1-11-1002	2,423.00
1379	13/06/01	HAN564	CR1 6TY	Boxed fireworks	2-21-1002	760.30
1380	14/06/01	MOD864	GU8 2ER	Flares	1-10-1001	11,265.00
1381	14/06/01	MOD421	BN4 2SA	Decoys	1-12-1001	19,650.00
1382	14/06/01	LEP043	SO14 3DT	Display fireworks	2-20-1001	2,398.85
1383	14/06/01	KMA149	Sweden	Flares	1-11-1001	20,800.00
1384	14/06/01	STE588	BH24 1SL	Warning rockets	1-10-1001	1,478.60
1385	14/06/01	HAN564	CR1 6TY	Boxed fireworks	2-21-1001	602.95
1386	14/06/01	AUD832	France	Display fireworks	1-11-2002	3,360.00
1387	15/06/01	MOD607	ED9 6TJ	Decoys	1-10-1001	17,342.00
1388	15/06/01	MAM001	9	Maroons	2-22-1011	1,580.00
1389	15/06/01	DOD930	Canada	Flares	1-11-1002	7,275.90
1390	15/06/01	AND476	OX5 4KN	Display fireworks	2-20-1201	2,876.50
1391	16/06/01	HAN564	CR1 6TY	Boxed fireworks	2-21-1001	326.90
1392	16/06/01	HAN564	CR1 6TY	Decoys	1-10-1001	1,563.90
1393	16/06/01	DDE089	Sri Lanka	Warning rockets	2-21-1001	5,240.00
1394	16/06/01	AUB623	DL8 21GR	Boxed fireworks	2-21-1001	1,487.85
1395	16/06/01	GUM991	Norway	Maroons	1-21-1002	2,225.00
1396	16/06/01	KMA193	Denmark	Warning rockets	1-11-1002	870.60
1397	16/06/01	MOA227	Saudi Arabia	Decoys	1-11-1002	14,768.00
Total						175,347.00

Pyropraktek Ltd - Payroll summary - Sheet 5 of 10 - Week 11 2001-02

Payroll number	Name	Job	Shift	Hours	Rate per hour £	Gross pay £
33/1071	I Lambert	Guard	Early	40.0	6.00	240.00
33/2126	P N McGee	Guard	Early	32.0	6.00	192.00
33/2158	A Ahmed	Fire fighter	Nights	40.0	12.00	480.00
33/2182	J D Hilder	Guard	Early	48.0	6.00	288.00
33/3213	C Jervis	Fire fighter	Late	40.0	10.00	400.00
33/3213	C Jervis	Fire fighter	Early	16.0	8.00	128.00
33/3309	M O Beatty	Guard	Nights	44.0	9.00	396.00
33/3378	R Singh	Guard	Late	44.0	7.50	330.00
33/3425	F F Evans	Fire fighter	Early	40.0	8.00	320.00
33/3515	E N Correy	Guard	Late	36.0	7.50	270.00
33/3515	E N Correy	Guard	Nights	48.0	9.00	432.00
33/3723	K Parker	Fire fighter	Nights	40.0	12.00	480.00
	TOTAL			468.00		3,956.00

Performance reports for the M&M division - May 2001

Profit centre	M&M UK sales		M&M Overseas sales		Total Division	
	Budget	Actual	Budget	Actual	Budget	Actual
	£'000	£'000	£'000	£'000	£'000	£'000
Sales	147.0	147.0	171.0	171.0	318.0	318.0
Variable costs:						
Direct materials	47.2	49.0	36.8	35.9	84.0	84.9
Internal purchases	16.8	22.4	22.2	29.6	39.0	52.0
Packaging	12.0	11.5	14.0	13.5	26.0	25.0
Direct wages	27.0	26.0	30.0	31.5	57.0	57.5
Total variable costs	103.0	108.9	103.0	110.5	206.0	219.4
Contribution	44.0	38.1	68.0	60.5	112.0	98.6

Performance reports for the E&R division - May 2001

Profit centre	E&R Direct sales		E&R Retailer sales		E&R Internal sales		Total Division	
	Budget	Actual	Budget	Actual	Budget	Actual	Budget	Actual
	£'000	£'000	£'000	£'000	£'000	£'000	£'000	£'000
Sales	95.4	95.5	142.7	142.6	39.0	52.0	277.1	290.1
Variable costs:								
Direct materials	32.3	31.8	53.3	52.8	15.0	14.9	100.6	99.5
Packaging	3.4	3.2	12.8	13.0	3.0	3.2	19.2	19.4
Direct wages	28.6	28.9	44.2	44.7	8.0	7.9	80.8	81.5
Total variable costs	64.3	63.9	110.3	110.5	26.0	26.0	200.6	200.4
Contribution	31.1	31.6	32.4	32.1	13.0	26.0	76.5	89.7

Answer (Task 1)

Pyropraktek Ltd - Sales invoice corrections sheets w/e						
Invoice no.	Date	Customer account no.	UK post code; Country; 9 = internal sales	Product	Account code	£

MEMO

To:

From:

c.c.

Date:

Subject:

Answer (Task 3)

SERIAN EXPLOSIVES PLC

**Leman House
38 Malzor St
New Hurdcott
Wiltshire SP17 7YF**

SALES INVOICE

Purchase invoice 7034
Account code...................................

To:
Pyropraktek Ltd (attn. Steve O'Connell)
Dutton Plain
Dutton, Hants S019 3QR

Invoice No:	6032/9
Account No:	PY00178
Date/Tax Pt:	10/06/01
Customer's order No:	MM2871

	kg	@	£
Propellant SR16	500	£97.00	48,500.00
Accelerator SR08	150	£132.00	19,800.00
Powder SR01	690	£41.20	28,428.00
Total goods			96,728.00
VAT @ 17.5%			16,927.40
Total due			113,655.40

VAT Reg: 6 935 6 072

SERIAN EXPLOSIVES PLC

Leman House
38 Malzor St
New Hurdcott
Wiltshire SP17 7YF

SALES INVOICE

Purchase invoice 7035
Account code.................................

To:
Pyropraktek Ltd (attn. Ledward Bayley)
Dutton Plain
Dutton, Hants S019 3QR

Invoice No:	6048/9
Account No:	PY00178
Date/Tax Pt:	13/06/01
Customer's order No:	ER5831

	kg	@	£
Propellant SR62	470	£53.00	24,910.00
Powder SR17	50	£31.65	1,582.50
Total goods			26,492.50
VAT @ 17.5%			4,636.19
Total due			31,128.69

VAT Reg: 6 935 6 072

Cranley Chase Chemicals plc

Forest Way - Harrow Middx - HA3 9YA

INVOICE

Customer:
Pyropraktek Ltd
(attention L Bayley)
Dutton Plain
DUTTON,
Hampshire
S019 3QR

Invoice No:	57554
Sheet No.	1 of 1
Account No:	478PYRO
Date/Tax Pt:	07/06/01
Customer's order No:	ER5833

Purchase invoice 7036
Account code...

	kg	@	£
Na	13.50	46.85	632.47
Mg	27.00	132.90	3,588.30
Fe	8.50	16.80	142.80
Powdered carbon	75.00	8.46	634.50
Zn	9.30	23.74	220.78
Total			5,218.85
VAT @ 17.5%			913.30
Total inc. VAT			6,132.15

VAT Reg: 3 191 2179

BPP PUBLISHING

Gleeson Containers Ltd

Pyropraktek Ltd
Dutton Plain
Dutton
Hants
SO19 3QR

Unit 8, Glebe Trading Estate
Peaceminster
Dorset BH32 9ED

VAT Reg: 4 283 3 071

For attention of: Carlyle
Duggan

SALES INVOICE: 329-7683

Purchase invoice 7037
Account code......................

Customer order number		ER5829	
Account number		11/32P	
Date & tax point		03 Jun 2001	

Cardboard tubing 5 cm dia. 2 m lengths	50	@ £3.64	£182.00

Goods total	£182.00
VAT @ 17.5%	£31.85
Total due	£213.85

Scottish & General Insurance

SGI House
Blackrigg
Appleby in Westmoreland
Cumbria
CU8 4FG

Premium advice

Purchase invoice 7038
Account code...............................

Pyropraktek Ltd
Dutton Plain
Dutton, Hants
S019 3QR

Account no:	63/8712
Advice no:	34-1879
Policy no.	113-56-7274
Date:	9 June 2001

Employers' liability insurance 1 July 2001 to 30 June 2002	£13,582.00
(For the attention of Company Secretary)	
Due by 30 June 2001	£13,582.00

Gleeson Containers Ltd

Pyropraktek Ltd
Dutton Plain
Dutton
Hants
SO19 3QR

Unit 8, Glebe Trading Estate
Peaceminster
Dorset BH32 9ED

VAT Reg: 4 283 3 071

For attention of: Cythia Rose

SALES INVOICE: 329-7692

Purchase invoice 7039
Account code...........................

	Customer order number	MM2865
	Account number	11/32P
	Date & tax point	04 Jun 2001

Grey plastic tubes 875 mm dia. 1 m length As per specification: PyroSpec/820013	200	@ £7.68	£1,536.00
Red plastic caps for 875 mm tube As per specification: PryrSpec/820014	400	@ £1.50	£600.00
Goods total VAT @ 17.5%			£2,136.00 £373.80
Total due			£2,509.80

Lancing Quigley Protection Ltd

42 Merchants Lane
Guildford
Surrey GU4 6TT

INVOICE

Purchase invoice 7040
Account code................................

Sandra Henman Pyropraktek Ltd Dutton Plain Dutton, Hants S019 3QR	Account No:	7437
	Invoice No:	Z999
	Date/Tax Pt:	12/06/01
	Customer's order	AS8502

Half-yearly check on fire extinguishers	138	@ £6.00	£828.00
Check fire alarm circuits			£1,500.00
Inspect sprinkler systems			£700.00
Total			£3,028.00
VAT @ 17.5%			£529.90
Due			£3,557.90

VAT Reg: 8 942 4171

BPP PUBLISHING

GOSSFERRY LTD

**166 Endless Street, New Hurdcott
Wiltshire SP17 6TT**

SALES INVOICE

Purchase invoice 7041
Account code...............................

To:
Pyropraktek Ltd (attn. Maurice Tan)
Dutton Plain
Dutton, Hants S019 3QR

Invoice No:	7429
Account No:	P048
Date/Tax Pt:	30/05/01
Customer's order No:	DD7367

Car(s) and date(s):	Miles	@ per mile	£
1. Scorpio V221 PLN (15 May '01) *(driving Mr Tan to Cardiff)*	334	£1.15	384.10

Driver(s)	Hours	@ per hour	
1. P Ledburn	8.0	£11.00	88.00

Total	472.10
VAT @ 17.5%	82.62
Due	554.72

VAT Reg: 3 395 0721

Scottish & General Insurance

**SGI House
Blackrigg
Appleby in Westmoreland
Cumbria
CU8 4FG**

Premium advice

Purchase invoice 7042
Account code...............................

Pyropraktek Ltd
Dutton Plain
Dutton, Hants
S019 3QR

Account no:	63/8712
Advice no:	67-7492
Policy no:	209-43-3187
Date:	9 June 2001

Buildings insurance 1 July 2001 to 30 June 2002 .... £18,750.00

(For the attention of Company Secretary)

Due by 30 June 2001 .... £18,750.00

DUTTON HERALD & CHRONICLE

Stangate House - Stangate - Dutton - SO14 1SL

VAT Reg: 3 191 2179

CLASSIFIED ADVERTISING

Attention: G Zemenides
Pyropraktek Ltd
Dutton Plain
DUTTON,
Hampshire SO19 3QR

Invoice No:	C/00/06/06/51
Customer's order No:	AS8519
Account No:	92/C/5482
Date/Tax Pt:	08/06/01

Purchase invoice 7043
Account code.................................

	£
Recruitment advertisement for night shift staff Dutton Herald & Chronicle - 6 June 2001 ¼ page	 500.00
	500.00
VAT @ 17.5%	87.50
Total inc. VAT	587.50

Each of the above purchase invoices has been stamped with a unique serial number. Within the box containing the purchase invoice serial number there is a space in which to enter the account code.

71

Answer (Task 4)

MEMO
To:
From:
c.c.
Date:
Subject:

Answer (Task 5)

Pyropraktek Ltd - Payroll posting slip - Gross wages				
Pay week	Account code	Hours	£	Notes

Answer (Task 6)

MEMO

To:

From:

c.c.

Date:

Subject:

Trial run devolved assessment 2: Gossferry Ltd

Trial run devolved assessment 2: Gossferry Ltd

Performance criteria

The following performance criteria are covered in this trial run devolved assessment

Element 4.1 Code and extract information

(i)   Appropriate cost centres and elements of cost are recognised

(ii)   Income and expenditure details are extracted from the relevant sources

(iii)   Income and expenditure are coded correctly

(iv)   Any problems in obtaining the necessary information are referred to the appropriate person

(v)   Errors are identified and reported to the appropriate person

Element 4.2 Provide comparisons on costs and income

(ii)   Information extracted from a particular source is compared with actual results

(iii)   Discrepancies are identified

(iv)   Comparisons are provided to the appropriate person in the required format

(v)   Organisation requirements for confidentiality are strictly followed

Notes on completing this trial run devolved assessment

This assessment is designed to test your ability to code and check financial data taken from sales invoices, purchase invoices and payroll records.

You are provided with all the necessary information and data to perform the specified tasks.

You are allowed 3 hours to complete your work

Please check your work carefully as complete accuracy is required.

You should work in black ink or biro – NOT in pencil. Errors should be crossed out neatly and clearly.

THE SITUATION

You are employed by Gossferry Ltd, a company operating a hire car business providing chauffeur driven cars to business clients.

One of your tasks is to code (or check the coding of) sales invoices, purchase invoices and payroll entries taken from Gossferry Ltd's financial accounting system for entry into a separate costing system. You are also expected to check the accuracy of actual costs by carrying out comparisons between forecast and actual costs and revenues.

Gossferry Ltd has three cost centres:

(a)   **Sales,** (manager Pietro Argenti).

(b)   **Vehicle maintenance,** (manager Wendy Bishop).

(c)   **Administration,** (manager Linda St. Helens).

Gossferry Ltd's business falls into three categories

(a)   **Contract hire** - car(s) and driver(s) hired for a minimum of two weeks.

(b)   **Account trade** - car(s) and driver(s) hired on a frequent but unpredictable basis. Customers are invoiced monthly for any account hirings.

(c)   **Occasional trade** - customers are invoiced each time they hire a car and driver. These customers do not have a personal account in the sales ledger - all **Occasional trade** invoices are posted to one account number, Z999.

Some customers' invoices may be coded as part **contract hire** and part **account trade**.

Each business category forms a profit centre to which revenue is credited and fuel and drivers' wages are charged. All other vehicle running costs (including vehicle insurance and licensing costs) are charged to Vehicle maintenance, while the non-wage costs of drivers are charged to Administration.

Drivers are only paid when they are working, so drivers' working hours and the hours charged to clients in a period should be the same.

Cars are charged at a rate per mile. Drivers' time is charged at an hourly rate. When a car is used, it is company policy to refill its tank with fuel at the end of each day. If possible fuel is purchased from 3 Bridges Filling Station which is close to Gossferry Ltd.

Gossferry Ltd have the following cars.

• Jaguar T337 HOW	On contract hire to Sarpennent & Ivory
• Lexus V918 PTB	On contract hire to Sarpennent & Ivory
• Mercedes P212 WER	On contract hire to Pearly Madness
• Rolls P777 HAC	Usually hired for weddings
• Lexus T341 FGH	For Account and Occasional hirings
• Scorpio V221 PLN	For Account and Occasional hirings

Gossferry Ltd employs the following drivers on a permanent basis.

• J Boddington
• C Jennings

P Ledburn and S Ahmed are employed as casual drivers.

Gossferry Ltd - Costing system coding sheet:

	Code
Profit centre codes:	
Contract hire	1
Account trade	2
Occasional trade	3
Cost centre codes:	
Sales	4
Vehicle maintenance	5
Administration	6
Suspense	9
Costing account codes:	
Sales revenue:	
Mileage charges	10
Driver charges	11
Vehicle running costs:	
Fuel	20
Brake, steering, & automatic gearbox fluid	21
Oil	22
Tyres	23
Motor parts	24
Servicing and repair charges	25
Vehicle insurance	26
Vehicle licensing	27
Vehicle valeting and cleaning materials	28
Employment costs:	
Drivers' wages	30
Staff salaries	31
Employers' national insurance	32
Employers' liability insurance	33
Personal accident insurance for drivers	34
Subsistence payments to drivers	35
Space costs and other expenses:	
Office rent	40
Cleaning contract	41
Business rates	42
Gas	43
Electricity	44
Telephone	45
Stationery	46
Parking and speeding fines	47
Advertising	50
Costing suspense account	99

Code items which cannot be allocated are coded to cost centre 9 and costing account Code 99.

All sales invoices, purchase invoices, payroll figures and any costing journal entries are recorded onto pre-numbered **costing system data entry sheets** from which they are entered into a computerised costing system.

THE TASKS TO BE COMPLETED

1   (a)   Code and enter the sales invoices on pages 81 to 83 into the relevant fields of the costing system data entry sheet on page 86.

      (b)   Check that the total of the values put on the data entry sheet corresponds to the sum of the invoice values before VAT.

2   Each purchase invoice is stamped with a serial number when it is received by Gossferry Ltd.

      Gossferry Ltd's computerised purchase ledger system provides a **day book** report which lists the details of all purchase invoices processed in the current period. This is shown on page 83.

      (a)   Code and enter the purchase invoice details contained in the purchase ledger day book report onto the costing system data entry sheet on page 86.

      (b)   Code the invoice for fuel to the costing suspense account.

      (c)   Code any other items of which you are uncertain to the costing suspense account.

3   In order to prevent data errors which have been detected being left uncorrected and also to highlight data queries Gossferry Ltd uses an **Error/Query report form**. Any errors or queries identified during the compilation of data entry sheets must be reported to the appropriate manager within Gossferry Ltd who will note on the form the action taken to resolve the error.

      Complete an Error/Query report form for each of the items you coded to the costing suspense account in Task 2 (except for the last item, fuel) so as to bring them to the correct managers' attention. Use the Error/Query report forms on page 87.

4   (a)   Code and enter 3 Bridges Filling Station's invoice on page 84 (purchase invoice serial number 01839) into the relevant fields of the costing system data entry sheets on page 88.

      (b)   Enter the total of the sheet as a negative figure and code this value to the costing suspense account.

      (c)   You should refer to the related sales invoices from Task 1 to ensure that your coding is correct.

5   (a)   Compare the data contained in the drivers' wages input sheet for June 2001 on page 84 with the data contained on each sales invoice for the month (see Task 1).

      (b)   Make a note of any data which appears to be incorrect or questionable.

      (c)   Complete the Error/Query report form on page 89.

6   (a)   Code and enter the relevant details from the drivers' wages input sheet on page 84 onto the costing system data entry sheet on page 89.

      (b)   Date each entry as 30/06/01.

7   (a) Compare the **total** actual costs for fuel and for drivers' wages with the forecast on page 85.

      (b) Report your findings to Linda St. Helens, copy to Pietro Argenti (use the blank memo on page 90).

      (c) Some of the matters that you may raise in your report are likely to be sensitive and would need to be treated as confidential. Explain how you would ensure that confidentiality is preserved.

DATA

GOSSFERRY LTD 166 Endless Street, New Hurdcott Wiltshire SP17 6TT	**SALES INVOICE**		
To: Sarpennent & Ivory Lomax House, 32 Milton St New Hurdcott SP17 3AU	Invoice No: 7435 Account No: S041 Date/Tax Pt: 30/06/01 Customer's order No: 99/4257		
Car(s) and date(s):	**Miles**	**@ per mile**	**£**
1. Jaguar T337 HOW (1 - 30 June 2001) 2. Lexus V918 PTB (1 - 30 June 2001) 3.	1,498 1,916	£1.60 £1.40	2,396.80 2,682.40
Driver(s)	**Hours**	**@ £ per hr**	
1. J Boddington 2. C Jennings 3.	220.0 192.0	£12.00 £11.00	2,640.00 2,112.00
Total			9,831.20
VAT @ 17.5%			1,720.46
Due			11,551.66
VAT Reg: 3 395 0721			

GOSSFERRY LTD

166 Endless Street, New Hurdcott

Wiltshire SP17 6TT

SALES INVOICE

To:			
Floating Ltd			
Unit 4, Freedom Trading Estate			
Shastonbury, Wilts			

Invoice No:	7436	
Account No:	Z999	
Date/Tax Pt:	19/06/01	
Customer's order No:	PD – 712/9	

Car(s) and date(s):	Miles	@ per mile	£
1. Scorpio V221 PLN (17 & 18 June 2001)	523	£1.15	601.45
2.			
3.			
Driver(s)	**Hours**	**@ per hour**	
1. P Ledburn	73.0	£20.50	1,496.50
2.			
3.			
Total			2,097.95
VAT @ 17.5%			367.14
Due			2,465.09

VAT Reg: 3 395 0721

GOSSFERRY LTD

166 Endless Street, New Hurdcott
Wiltshire SP17 6TT

SALES INVOICE

To:			
P J Lewmar Esq.			
81, Roning Ave			
New Hurdcott SP17 3FG			

Invoice No:	7437	
Account No:	Z999	
Date/Tax Pt:	12/06/00	
Customer's order No:	tel. 7/06/01	

Car(s) and date(s):	Miles	@ per mile	£
1. Rolls P777 HAC (10 June 2001)	33	£5.75	189.75
2.			
3.			
Driver(s)	**Hours**	**@ per hour**	
1. P Ledburn	6.0	£20.50	123.00
2.			
3.			
Total			312.75
VAT @ 17.5%			54.73
Due			367.48

VAT Reg: 3 395 0721

GOSSFERRY LTD

166 Endless Street, New Hurdcott
Wiltshire SP17 6TT

SALES INVOICE

To:
Hanly, Evans & Bright
8 Manor Rd, Mewdon
Wilts

Invoice No:	7438
Account No:	H048
Date/Tax Pt:	30/06/01
Customer's order No:	73-671

Car(s) and date(s):	Miles	@ per mile	£
1. Scorpio V221 PLN (1 June 2001)	156	£1.15	179.40
2. Scorpio V221 PLN (7 June 2001)	94	£1.15	108.10
3. Lexus T341 4FGH (28 June 2001)	203	£1.40	284.20
Driver(s)	**Hours**	**@ per hour**	
1. P Ledburn	8.0	£11.00	88.00
2. S Ahmed	4.5	£11.00	49.50
3. S Ahmed	9.5	£11.00	104.50
Total			813.70
VAT @ 17.5%			142.40
Due			956.10

VAT Reg: 3 395 0721

Gossferry Ltd - Purchase ledger day book report - 30 June 2001

Invoice serial no.	Invoice date	Suppliers' account no.	Details	Net £	VAT £	Gross £
01831	26/06/01	J0346	Tyres - Lexus V918 PTB	400.00	70.00	470.00
01832	26/06/01	Q0409	Repair - Scorpio V221 PLN	550.00	96.25	646.25
01833	27/06/01	B1298	Vehicle cleaning materials	83.60	14.63	98.23
01834	30/06/01	B0347	Telephone - June 2000	439.75	76.96	516.71
01835	30/06/01	G0980	Speeding fine - P Ledburn	400.00	0	400.00
01836	30/06/01	R0087	Music CDs for in car use	50.00	8.75	58.75
01837	30/06/01	Y1801	$^{1}/_{2}$ page advert - Motor News	875.00	153.12	1,028.12
01838	30/06/01	A2045	Optician's fee - P Ledburn	40.00	0	40.00
01839	30/06/01	30001	Fuel w/e 30 June 2001	381.78	66.81	448.59
			TOTAL	3,220.13	486.52	3,706.65

3 Bridges Filling Station - Marks Roundabout - New Hurdcott, Wilts SP17 3QA

FUEL INVOICE

Gossferry Ltd 166 Endless Street New Hurdcott, Wilts SP17 6TT	Invoice No: 765554 Sheet No: 1 of 1 Account No: GOS/478 Date/Tax Pt: 30/06/01 Customer's order No: 020356

Petrol & diesel supplied week ended 30/6/01	**Purchase invoice serial no. 01839**

Vehicle and registration number:	Date	Litres	£
Jaguar T337 HOW	24/06/01	27.1	24.39
Rolls - P777 HAC	24/06/01	15.0	13.50
Lexus - T341 4FGH	24/06/01	7.0	6.30
Mercedes P212 WER	24/06/01	26.4	23.76
Mercedes P212 WER	25/06/01	27.8	25.02
Lexus - V918 PTB	26/06/01	19.0	17.10
Jaguar T337 HOW	26/06/01	32.0	28.80
Lexus - V918 PTB	27/06/01	29.0	26.10
Jaguar T337 HOW	27/06/01	14.0	12.60
Mercedes P212 WER	27/06/01	29.4	26.46
Lexus - T341 4FGH	28/06/01	35.0	31.50
Mercedes P212 WER	28/06/01	31.2	28.08
Lexus - V918 PTB	28/06/01	8.0	7.20
Lexus - V918 PTB	29/06/01	31.0	27.90
Mercedes P212 WER	29/06/01	26.3	23.67
Jaguar T337 HOW	29/06/01	17.0	15.30
Lexus - V918 PTB	30/06/01	6.0	5.40
Jaguar T337 HOW	30/06/01	43.0	38.70
Total fuel		424.20	381.78
VAT @ 17.5%			66.81
Total inc. VAT			448.59
VAT Reg: 6 915 1279			

The fuel supplied for 1-23 June, the cost of which excluding VAT was £1,105.65, has been invoiced on previous invoices.

Gossferry Ltd - Drivers' wages input sheet - June 2001						
Payroll entry number	Name	Pay No.	Hours	Rate per hr.	Gross pay	Notes
00/0108	J Boddington	438	220.0	6.00	1,320.00	Month
00/0109	C Jennings	302	192.0	5.50	1,056.00	Month
00/0110	P Ledburn	376	8.0	5.50	44.00	1 June
00/0111	P Ledburn	376	6.0	10.25	61.50	Sat 10 June
00/0112	P Ledburn	376	13.0	10.25	133.25	Sat/Sun17/18
00/0113	S Ahmed	421	4.5	5.50	24.75	7 June
00/0114	S Ahmed	421	9.5	5.50	52.25	28 June
	TOTAL		453.0		2,691.75	

Gossferry Ltd - Forecast gross profit - June 2001

Profit centre	Contract hire	Account trade	Occasional trade	Total
Miles	6,000	2,000	2,000	10,000
Litres fuel	1,200	400	400	2,000
Drivers' hours	300	60	60	420
	£	£	£	£
Revenue:				
Mileage	9,000	3,000	3,000	15,000
Drivers time	3,300	660	660	4,620
Total	12,300	3,660	3,660	19,620
Costs:				
Fuel	1,200	400	400	2,000
Drivers' wages	1,650	330	330	2,310
Total	2,850	730	730	4,310
Gross profit	9,450	2,930	2,930	15,310

BPP PUBLISHING

Answer (Task 1)

Gossferry Ltd - Costing system data entry sheet

Entry no.	Sales invoice no.	Purchase invoice serial no.	Payroll entry no.	Cost journal no.	Profit or cost centre code	Costing account code	Date	£
1301								
1302								
1303								
1304								
1305								
1306								
1307								
1308								
1309								
1310								
1311								
1312								
1313								
1314								
TOTAL								

Answer (Task 2)

Gossferry Ltd - Costing system data entry sheet

Entry no.	Sales invoice no.	Purchase invoice serial no.	Payroll entry no.	Cost journal no.	Profit or cost centre code	Costing account code	Date	£
1325								
1326								
1327								
1328								
1329								
1330								
1331								
1332								
1333								
1334								
1335								
Total								

Answer (Task 3)

Gossferry Ltd - Error/Query report form *(Note: only one error or query is to be entered on this report)*	Serial No: 2000/0144
To:	c.c.
Details of error/query	
From:	Date:
Action taken (to be completed by recipient):	

Gossferry Ltd - Error/Query report form *(Note: only one error or query is to be entered on this report)*	Serial No: 2000/0145
To:	c.c.
Details of error/query	
From:	Date:
Action (to be completed by recipient):	

Answer (Task 4)

Gossferry Ltd - Costing system data entry sheet

Entry no.	Sales invoice no.	Purchase invoice serial no.	Payroll entry no.	Cost journal no.	Profit or Cost centre code	Costing account code	Date	£
1401								
1402								
1403								
1404								
1405								
1406								
1407								
1408								
1409								
1410								
1411								
1412								
1413								
1414								
1415								
1416								
1417								
1418								
1419								
1420								
TOTAL								

Answer (Task 5)

Gossferry Ltd - Error/Query report form *(Note: only one error or query is to be entered on this report)*		Serial No:	2000/0146
To:	c.c.		
Details of error/query			
From	Date:		
Action taken (to be completed by recipient):			

Answer (Task 6)

Gossferry Ltd - Costing system data entry sheet

Entry no.	Sales invoice no.	Purchase invoice serial no.	Payroll entry no.	Cost journal no.	Profit or Cost centre code	Costing account code	Date	£
1421								
1422								
1423								
1424								
1425								
1426								
1427								
1428								
1429								
1430								
TOTAL								

Answer (Task 7)

MEMO

To:

From:

c.c.

Date:

Subject:

Answers to trial run devolved assessment 1: Pyropraktek Ltd

PROPRAKTEK LTD: ANSWERS

Task 1

Invoice no.	Date	Customer account no.	UK post code; Country; 9 = internal sales	Product	Account code	£
1374	12/06/01	MAM001	9	Warning rockets	2-22-1011	982.50
1375	13/06/01	KEN567	NW1 4QH	Display Fireworks	2-20-1001	1,370.00
1377	13/06/01	PID661	India	Maroons	1-11-1002	1,302.90
1379	13/06/01	HAN 564	CRI 6TY	Boxed Fireworks	2-21-1001	760.30
1381	14/06/01	MOD421	BN4 2SA	Decoys	1-10-1001	19,650.00
1383	14/06/01	KMA149	Sweden	Flares	1-11-1002	20,800.00
1386	14/06/01	AUD832	France	Display Fireworks	1-11-1002	3,360.00
1390	15/06/01	AND476	OX5 4KN	Display Fireworks	2-20-1001	2,876.50
1393	16/06/01	DDE089	Sri Lanka	Warning rockets	1-11-1002	5,240.00
1395	16/06/01	GUM991	Norway	Maroons	1-11-1002	2,225.00

The top of the table reads: **Pyropraktek Ltd - Sales invoice corrections sheet w/e 17 June 2001**

Task 2

MEMO

To: Chris Jones
From: A Student
c.c.   Naomi Bloom
Date: 21 June 2001

Subject: Possible coding error on sales invoice

Invoice numbers 1391 and 1392 are both to the same customer, account number HAN564. Invoice 1391 is for boxed fireworks while invoice 1392 is for decoys. It seems strange that the same customer should be purchasing these two very different items, particularly as decoys should only be sold to military customers.

Invoices 1385 and 1379 are also for boxed fireworks to customer HAN564, so it would appear that invoice 1392 has been given the wrong customer account number or the wrong product description.

Could you please investigate and advise me of what action to take.

A Technician

Task 3

Purchase invoice 7034 *Account code........1/13/2001..........*	*Purchase invoice 7035* *Account code.......2/23/2001...........*
Purchase invoice 7036 *Account code......2/23/2001.............*	*Purchase invoice 7037* *Account code......2/24/2002.............*
Purchase invoice 7038 *Account code......3/30/3101.............*	*Purchase invoice 7039* *Account code......1/15/2002.............*
Purchase invoice 7040 *Account code......3/33/5005.............*	*Purchase invoice 7041* *Account code......4/40/5021.............*
Purchase invoice 7042 *Account code......3/30/5001.............*	*Purchase invoice 7043* *Account code......3/36/5031.............*

Task 4

MEMO

To: Brenda Magumbe
From: A Technician
c.c.   Mina Nathwani
Date: 21 June 2001

Subject: Apportionment of employers' liability insurance

The premium for employers' liability insurance for 1 July 2001 to 30 June 2002 has to be apportioned between profit and cost centres using their wages and salaries bill for May 2001 as a basis.

Could you please let me have the wages and salaries figures for each profit and cost centre for May 2001.

In order to preserve the confidentiality of the data it would be helpful if you could give me each profit centre and cost centre's wages and salaries bill as a percentages of the total wages and salaries bill. Alternatively, I could work on the payroll data in your office, without taking copies.

A Technician

Task 5

Pyropraktek Ltd - Payroll posting slip - Gross wages				
Pay week	**Account code**	**Hours**	**£**	**Notes**
11	3-33-3011	292	2,148.00	*E N Correy has worked on the late and the night shift.*
11	3-34-3011	176	1,808.00	*C Jervis has worked on the late and the early shift.*

Task 6

MEMO

To: Joan Degas and Alexander Surtees
From: A Technician
c.c.   Patrick Connelly; Chris Jones; Leslie Edge
Date: 21 June 2001

Subject: May 2001 Performance Reports, M&M and E&R Divisions

The actual contribution for the M&M Division in May 2001 is £13,400 (12%) below budget. The actual contribution for the E&R Division in May 2001 is £13,200 (17%) above budget.

The reason for these discrepancies is that internal sales made by E&R to M&M are £13,000 higher than budget.

A Technician

Answers to trial run devolved assessment 2: Gossferry Ltd

GOSSFERRY LTD: ANSWERS

Task 1

Gossferry Ltd - Costing system data entry sheet							
Entry no.	Sales invoice no.	Purchase invoice serial no.	Payroll entry no.	Costing journal no.	Profit or Cost centre code	Costing account code	Date	£
1301	7435				1	10	30/06/01	2,396.80
1302	7435				1	10	30/06/01	2,682.40
1303	7435				1	11	30/06/01	2,640.00
1304	7435				1	11	30/06/01	2,112.00
1305	7436				3	10	30/06/01	601.45
1306	7436				3	11	30/06/01	1,496.50
1307	7437				3	10	30/06/01	189.75
1308	7437				3	11	30/06/01	123.00
1309	7438				2	10	30/06/01	179.40
1310	7438				2	10	30/06/01	108.10
1311	7438				2	10	30/06/01	284.20
1312	7438				2	11	30/06/01	88.00
1313	7438				2	11	30/06/01	49.50
1314	7438				2	11	30/06/01	104.50
TOTAL								13,055.60

Task 2

Gossferry Ltd - Costing system data entry sheet							
Entry no.	Sales invoice no.	Purchase invoice serial no.	Payroll entry no.	Cost journal no.	Profit or Cost centre code	Costing account code	Date	£
1325		01831			5	23	26/06/01	400.00
1326		01832			5	25	26/06/01	550.00
1327		01833			5	28	27/06/01	83.60
1328		01834			6	45	30/06/01	439.75
1329		01835			6	47	30/06/01	400.00
1330		01836			9	99	30/06/01	50.00
1331		01837			4	50	30/06/01	875.00
1332		01838			9	99	30/06/01	40.00
1333		01839			9	99	30/06/01	381.78
1334								
1335								
TOTAL								3,220.13

BPP PUBLISHING

Task 3

Gossferry Ltd. - Error/Query report form *(Note: only one error or query is to be entered on this report)*	Serial No: 2000/0144
To: *Wendy Bishop*	c.c. *Linda St. Helens*
Details of error/query *Invoice Serial No 01836 for £50 plus Vat relates to 'Music CDs for in car use'. I am uncertain as to how I should code this item as there does not appear to be a suitable costing account code.* *Would you please advise me.*	
From: *A Technician*	Date: *4 July 2001*
Action taken (to be completed by recipient):	

Gossferry Ltd. - Error/Query report form *(Note: only one error or query is to be entered on this report)*	Serial No: 2000/0145
To: *Linda St. Helens*	c.c.
Details of error/query *Invoice Serial No. 01838 refers to 'Opticians fee - P Ledburn'. I am not sure how I should code this as there does not appear to be a suitable costing account code.* *Please advise*	
From: *A Technician*	Date: *4 July 2001*
Action (to be completed by recipient):	

BPP PUBLISHING

Task 4

Gossferry Ltd - Costing system data entry sheet

Entry no.	Sales invoice no.	Purchase invoice serial no.	Payroll entry no.	Cost journal no.	Profit or Cost centre code	Costing account code	Date	£
1401		01839			1	20	24/06/01	24.39
1402		01839			3	20	24/06/01	13.50
1403		01839			3	20	24/06/01	6.30
1404		01839			1	20	24/06/01	23.76
1405		01839			1	20	25/06/01	25.02
1406		01839			1	20	26/06/01	17.10
1407		01839			1	20	26/06/01	28.80
1408		01839			1	20	27/06/01	26.10
1409		01839			1	20	27/06/01	12.60
1410		01839			1	20	27/06/01	26.46
1411		01839			2	20	28/06/01	31.50
1412		01839			1	20	28/06/01	28.08
1413		01839			1	20	28/06/01	7.20
1414		01839			1	20	29/06/01	27.90
1415		01839			1	20	29/06/01	23.67
1416		01839			1	20	29/06/01	15.30
1417		01839			1	20	30/06/01	5.40
1418		01839			1	20	30/06/01	38.70
1419		01839			9	99	30/06/01	-381.78
1420								
TOTAL								0

Task 5

Gossferry Ltd. - Error/Query report form (*Note: only one error or query is to be entered on this report*)	Serial No: 2000/0146
To: *Pietro Argenti*	c.c. *Linda St Helens*

Details of error/query

Sales invoice 7436 relates to hiring Scorpio V221 PLN to Floating Ltd on Saturday and Sunday 17 and 18 June 2001 with P Ledburn as the driver. The invoice shows 73 driver hours whereas the drivers' wages input sheet for June 2001 shows 13 hours. The figure of 73 hours on the invoice appears to be incorrect as it is an impossible figure for only two days (48 hour max).

From: *A Technician*	Date: *4 July 2001*

Action taken (to be completed by recipient):

Task 6

Gossferry Ltd - Costing system data entry sheet

Entry no.	Sales invoice no.	Purchase invoice serial no.	Payroll entry no.	Cost journal no.	Profit or Cost centre code	Costing account code	Date	£
1421			00/0108		1	30	30/06/01	1,320.00
1422			00/0109		1	30	30/06/01	1,056.00
1423			00/0110		2	30	30/06/01	44.00
1424			00/0111		3	30	30/06/01	61.50
1425			00/0112		3	30	30/06/01	133.25
1426			00/0113		2	30	30/06/01	24.75
1437			00/0114		2	30	30/06/01	52.25
1428								
1429								
1430								
TOTAL								2,691.75

Task 7

MEMO

To: Linda St. Helens

From: A Technician

c.c. Pietro Argenti

Date: 4 July 2001

Subject: Comparison between June 2001 forecast costs for fuel and drivers' wages and the actual costs.

CONFIDENTIAL

Item	Forecast	Actual	Discrepancy
Fuel	£2,000	£1,487	Actual £513 *below* forecast
Wages	£2,310	£2,692	Actual £382 *above* forecast

A Technician

As this memo contains confidential material I would either hand it to Linda St. Helens and Pietro Argenti personally, or I would put it in an envelope marked 'Private and Confidential'.

AAT Sample Simulation

DATA AND TASKS

INSTRUCTIONS

This simulation is designed to test your ability to supply information for management control.

This situation is set out on pages 106 and 107.

The tasks that you are required to complete are set out on page 108.

This simulation also requires data that you will need to complete the tasks. You should read the whole simulation before commencing work so as to gain an overall picture of what is required.

Your answers should be set out in the answer booklet on pages 117 - 124.

You are allowed **three hours** to complete your work.

A high level of accuracy is required. Check your work carefully before handing it in.

Correcting fluid may be used but it should be used in moderation. Errors should be crossed out neatly and clearly. You should write in ink, not pencil.

You are reminded that you should not bring any unauthorised material, such as books or notes, into the simulation. If you have any such material in your possession, you should surrender it to the assessor immediately.

Any instances of misconduct will be brought to the attention of the AAT, and disciplinary action may be taken.

Coverage of performance criteria and range statements

It should be recognised that it is not always possible to cover all performance criteria and range statements in a simulation; some may be more appropriate and entirely natural in the workplace and others may not be practicable within the scope of a particular simulation. Where performance criteria and range statements are not covered they must be assessed by other means by the assessor before a candidate can be deemed competent. Page 113 gives an indication of the performance criteria coverage for this simulation and also flags up the need to ensure that all areas of the range statements are covered.

A full answer to this simulation is provided on page 127.

BPP PUBLISHING

THE SITUATION

Your name is Candy Date and you work as an accounts assistant in the administration department of 'Cards-R-Us', a producer of greeting cards.

You report to the management accountant, Thelma Jones. Your work is on a monthly cycle with other projects being given to you by Thelma Jones at various times. Your main tasks are coding income and expenditure from all source documents and preparing performance reports. A junior assistant, Liam Green, sometimes helps you during busy periods.

Today's date is 12 September 2000.

'Cards-R-Us' makes three types of cards:

- Birthday cards
- Christmas cards
- Special occasion cards

Sales are recorded in the following profit centres:

- United Kingdom
- Europe
- USA
- Rest of world

Production is organised into the following cost centres:

- Printing
- Cutting
- Wrapping
- Packing

Production is serviced by the following cost centres:

- Administration
- Stores
- Marketing and distribution
- Maintenance

The coding system

The coding system for the company is based on three-digit system.

The first digit denotes the type of income or expenditure:

1   Profit centre income
2   Cost centre expenditure
3   Asset expenditure
4   Liabilities
5   Capital

Profit centres

The profit centres are coded as follows:

110	United Kingdom
120	Europe
130	USA
140	Rest of world

The third digit denotes the type of sale:

001	Birthday cards
002	Christmas cards
003	Special occasion cards

This means that the sale of birthday cards in Europe would be coded 121.

Cost centres

The cost centres are coded as follows:

210	Printing		250	Administration
220	Cutting		260	Stores
230	Wrapping		270	Marketing and distribution
240	Packing		280	Maintenance

The third digit denotes the type of expenditure:

001	Material
002	Labour
003	Expenses

This means that the rent expense of the wrapping department would be 233.

Performance reports

The performance reports that you prepare on a monthly basis are for the:

- Management accountant
- Sales director
- Production director
- Cost centre managers
- Profit centre managers

BPP PUBLISHING

THE TASKS TO BE COMPLETED

1   Refer to the sales and purchases invoices on pages 109-110.

    Code these invoices by completing the coding extract for income and expenditure on page 117. For each relevant code you should post the amendment and update the balance. Ignore the VAT element (this is coded automatically upon receipt of the invoice).

2   You receive the memo on page 111 from a cost centre manager about wage payment that has been missed on the packing department for the month of August 2000.

    Read the memo and then do the following:

- Complete the wage payment schedule on page 118 to the nearest penny.

- Amend the coding extract on page 117 and update the relevant codes to the nearest £.

    Note: Basic pay is coded to labour and other employee costs are coded to expenses.

3   Liam Green has left on your desk the three invoices shown on page 112 together with the note shown on page 111.

    Review the note and the three invoices and then write a memo to Liam Green using the blank memo paper on page 119. The memo should advise him:

- Of any mistakes in checking and coding that have been made.

- Of the appropriate persons that he needs to contact to get the information to carry out the correct coding.

    Date your memo for 12 September 2000.

4   On page 120 you will find a list of ledger balances for the year to date to 31 July 2000.

    Update this to 31 August 2000 by posting the amended coding extract that you have completed on page 117.

5   Using your answer from task 4, complete the performance report for total costs of the production cost centres on page 121 of the answer booklet.

6   Thelma has asked that you report to her any production cost variance of more than 10% from budget, either for the year to date or for the month of August 2000.

    Using your answer to task 5, complete the discrepancy (variance) report on page 122, and then use the comment section to identify the significant variances that Thelma has asked for.

7   Using your answer to task 4, complete the sales performance report for total sales on page 123.

8   Joan Standard, the Sales Director, is new to the post and the sales performance report that you completed in task 7 and sent to her is the first that she has received from you. Liam has taken a message from her asking you to phone her back to tell her:

- What you see as the key purpose of the report
- What uses it can be put to
- What other information can be provided from the date that you have available

    Using the notepad on page 124 list the key points that you see as the basis of the telephone conversation that you will have with her.

"CARDS R US"

SAFFRON DRIVE
WEST WALFORD
SALOPS
SA 4 9LK

VAT NO: 241162208
TEL NO: 07 421 316
FAX NO: 07 421 317
TAX POINT: 30 AUG 2000

SALES INVOICE

TO
CARD WAREHOUSE LTD
18 ROLLOVER DRIVE
TOSCAN
WORKBURG USA

INVOICE NO: 28417

DETAILS	NO.	NET £	TOTAL £
Type A Birthday Cards	2,000	0.80	1,600.00
Type C Wedding Cards	3,000	1.00	3,000.00
TOTAL BEFORE VAT			4,600.00
VAT			0.00
TOTAL INCLUDING VAT			4,600.00

"CARDS R US"

SAFFRON DRIVE
WEST WALFORD
SALOPS
SA 4 9LK

VAT NO: 241162208
TEL NO: 07 421 316
FAX NO: 07 421 317
TAX POINT: 30 AUG 2000

SALES INVOICE

TO
SURESHOP LTD
17 RUE DU PARIS
PARIS
FRANCE

INVOICE NO: 29124

DETAILS	NO.	NET £	TOTAL £
Type C Christmas Cards	2,000	0.85	1,700.00
Type D Engagement Cards	4,000	0.95	3,800.00
TOTAL BEFORE VAT			5,500.00
VAT			0.00
TOTAL INCLUDING VAT			5,500.00

BPP PUBLISHING

TRANWAY PRINTING

35 Holding Way
Whippleton
Leics
LE9 2NR

Invoice No:	6195
VAT No:	246 368 241
Tax Point:	30/08/2000
Tel No:	01567 78645
Fax No:	01567 78646

INVOICE TO
Cards R Us
Saffron Drive
West Walford
Salops
SA4 9LK

£

100 rolls of card at £8.90 per roll to be delivered to your Cutting Department	890.00
300 fabric prints at £2.50 per print to be delivered to your Print Department	750.00
VAT	287.00
Total including VAT	1,927.00

D. A. Associates

22 Catlin Road
York Avenue
Maidstone
Kent MA9 4CL

Invoice No:	2167
VAT No:	310 861 143
Tax Point:	26/08/2000
Tel No:	01234 862178
Fax No:	01234 862179

INVOICE TO
Cards R Us
Saffron Drive
West Walford
Salops
SA4 9LK

£

Maintenance Contract for the machines in your Wrapping Department For the year ending 31 July 2001	1,500.00
VAT	262.50
Total including VAT	1,762.50

MEMO

To: Candy Date, Accounts Assistant

From: John Steel, Packing Department Manager

Date: 11 September 2000

Subject: Missed wage payment

We missed a wage payment for John White, an operative on one of our packing machines, for the last week of August 2000. He worked 35 hours at a rate of £8 per hour and then did 8 hours of overtime at time and a half to clear a general backlog.

Please calculate and code the basic wage payment and employee costs and then pass the details on to the payroll department for the personal deductions. He is a full time employee so the employer's pension contribution of 6% of basic wage payment applies, as does the employer's national insurance contributions of 12½% above £84 per week.

Thanks

NOTEPAD

Candy

I have just checked and coded the attached invoices for September 2000 but I am not sure whether the action I have taken is correct. Please help!

Liam

Ince and Sons Brokers

2 Lambert Avenue
Bristol
BR9 6EL

Invoice No: 2167

Tel No: 01717 733451

Invoice to:
Cards R Us
Saffron Drive
West Walford
Salops
SA4 9LK

213

Provision of insurance for your factory for the year ending
30 September 2001

£6,000.00

Aftercare Limited

13 Carson Road
London
SN4 0EL

Invoice No: 1468
VAT No: 789 453 292
Tax Point: 11 September 2000
Tel No: 020 7941 367

Invoice to:
Cards Delight
27 Wapping Lane
Portsmouth
Hants
PO1 9FM

253

Provision of temporary staff for your Admin. Department
8 days at £150 per day

£1,200

Cellphate Ltd

Unit 6,
Dockway Drive,
Liverpool LA4 5XF

Invoice No: 4736

VAT No: 241 074 375
Tax Point: 4 September 2000
Tel No: 0151 441 857

Invoice to:
Cards R Us
Saffron Drive
West Walford
Salops
SA4 9LK

231

48 boxes of wrapping material at £25 per box

£12,000

COVERAGE OF THE PERFORMANCE CRITERIA

The following performance criteria are covered in this simulation in the tasks noted.

Element	PC Coverage	Task(s)
4.1	**Code and extract information**	
(i)	• Appropriate cost centres and elements of costs are recognised	1, 2
(ii)	• Income and expenditure details are extracted from the relevant sources	4
(iii)	• Income and expenditure are coded correctly	1, 2, 4
(iv)	• Any problems in obtaining the necessary information are referred to the appropriate person	3
(v)	• Errors are identified and reported to the appropriate person	3
4.2	**Provide comparisons on costs and income**	
(i)	• Information requirements are clarified with the appropriate person	8
(ii)	• Information extracted from a particular source is compared with actual results	5, 7
(iii)	• Discrepancies are identified	3, 6
(iv)	• Comparisons are provided to the appropriate person in the required format	5, 6, 7

BPP PUBLISHING

COVERAGE OF THE PERFORMANCE CRITERIA

The following performance criteria are covered in this simulation in the tasks noted.

Element	PC Coverage	Task(s)
4.1	Code and extract information	
(i)	• Appropriate cost centres and elements of costs are recognised	1, 2
(ii)	• Income and expenditure details are extracted from the relevant sources	1
(iii)	• Income and expenditure are coded correctly	1, 2, 4
(iv)	• Any problems in obtaining the necessary information are referred to the appropriate person	3
(v)	• Errors are identified and reported to the appropriate person	3
4.2	Provide comparisons on costs and income	
(i)	• Information requirements are clarified with the appropriate person	3
(ii)	• Information extracted from a particular source is compared with actual results	5, 7
(iii)	• Discrepancies are identified	6, 8
(iv)	• Comparisons are provided to the appropriate person in the required format	5, 7

Answer Booklet for AAT Sample Simulation

Answer Booklet for
AAT Sample
Simulation

ANSWERS (Tasks 1 and 2)

CODING EXTRACT: INCOME AND EXPENDITURE AUGUST 2000
(ROUNDED TO THE NEAREST £)

Code	Balance £	Amendment £	Updated balance £
111	38,916		
112	27,413		
113	33,476		
121	42,457		
122	29,376		
123	24,294		
131	38,461		
132	34,761		
133	37,314		
141	41,694		
142	52,316		
143	45,761		
211	47,412		
212	11,467		
213	20,439		
221	43,764		
222	11,461		
223	15,064		
231	8,216		
232	4,916		
233	9,074		
241	3,642		
242	4,164		
243	7,695		
253	6,613		
263	7,008		
273	6,744		
283	4,539		

BPP PUBLISHING

ANSWERS (Task 2)

PAYROLL CALCULATION AUGUST 2000			
NAME			
DEPARTMENT			
BASIC RATE			
HOURS WORKED			
HOURS FOR OVERTIME PREMIUM			
	Calculation	Amount (£)	Code
BASIC PAY			
OVERTIME PREMIUM			
EMPLOYERS PENSION CONT.			
EMPLOYERS N.I.C.			
TOTALS FOR POSTING	Code		Amount(£)

BPP PUBLISHING

ANSWERS (Task 3)

MEMO
To:
From:
Date:
Subject:

_____

_____

_____

_____

_____

_____

_____

_____

_____

_____

_____

_____

_____

_____

_____

_____

_____

_____

_____

_____

_____

_____

_____

BPP PUBLISHING

ANSWERS (Task 4)

INCOME AND EXPENDITURE BALANCES – Y/E 31/12/2000

Ledger Account	Bal. at 31/7/2000	Amt. Coded Aug 2000	Bal. at 31.8.2000
Sales	£	£	£
Birthday Cards			
- U.K.	245,365		
- Europe	198,467		
- U.S.A.	231,989		
- R. of W.	297,946		
Christmas Cards			
- U.K.	246,578		
- Europe	316,478		
- U.S.A.	297,697		
- R. of W.	399,906		
Special Cards			
- U.K.	198,464		
- Europe	201,897		
- U.S.A.	246,890		
- R. of W.	299,785		
Expenditure			
Printing			
- Material	74,789		
- Labour	61,890		
- Expenses	93,167		
Cutting			
- Material	71,789		
- Labour	58,625		
- Expenses	75,293		
Wrapping			
- Material	58,693		
- Labour	31,704		
- Expenses	34,471		
Packing			
- Material	38,568		
- Labour	36,906		
- Expenses	48,966		

ANSWERS (Task 5)

PERFORMANCE REPORT PRODUCTION COST CENTRES TOTAL COSTS – AUGUST 2000				
	MONTH – AUG 2000		YEAR TO DATE	
	Actual £	Budget £	Actual £	Budget £
Material		108,500		341,700
Labour		32,250		198,500
Expenses		48,750		277,100

ANSWERS (Task 6)

DISCREPANCY (VARIANCE) REPORT PRODUCTION COST CENTRES AUGUST 2000		
COST / PERIOD	MONTH £	YEAR TO DATE £
Material		
Labour		
Expenses		

COMMENT

ANSWERS (Task 7)

SALES PERFORMANCE REPORT – AUGUST 2000				
PERIOD PROFIT CENTRE	MONTH ACTUAL £	MONTH BUDGET £	YEAR TO DATE ACTUAL £	YEAR TO DATE BUDGET £
UNITED KINGDOM		98,000		785,000
EUROPE		109,000		832,500
U.S.A.		112,800		886,400
REST OF WORLD		142,100		1,164,600

BPP
PUBLISHING

ANSWERS (Task 8)

NOTEPAD

Key points for telephone conversation with Sales Director

Answers to AAT
Sample Simulation

ANSWERS (Tasks 1 and 2)

CODING EXTRACT: INCOME AND EXPENDITURE AUGUST 2000
(ROUNDED TO THE NEAREST £)

Code	Balance	Amendment	Updated balance
	£	£	£
111	38,916		38,916
112	27,413		27,413
113	33,476		33,476
121	42,457		42,457
122	29,376	1,700	31,076
123	24,294	3,800	28,094
131	38,461	1,600	40,061
132	34,761		34,761
133	37,314	3,000	40,314
141	41,694		41,694
142	52,316		52,316
143	45,761		45,761
211	47,412	750	48,162
212	11,467		11,467
213	20,439		20,439
221	43,764	890	44,654
222	11,461		11,461
223	15,064		15,064
231	8,216		8,216
232	4,916		4,916
233	9,074	1,500	10,574
241	3,642		3,642
242	4,164	344	4,508
243	7,695	89	7,784
253	6,613		6,613
263	7,008		7,008
273	6,744		6,744
283	4,539		4,539

BPP PUBLISHING

ANSWERS (Task 2)

PAYROLL CALCULATION AUGUST 2000			
NAME	JOHN WHITE		
DEPARTMENT	PACKING		
BASIC RATE	£8.00 PER HOUR		
HOURS WORKED	43		
HOURS FOR OVERTIME PREMIUM	8		
	Calculation	Amount (£)	Code
BASIC PAY	43hrs × £8	344.00	242★
OVERTIME PREMIUM	8hrs × £8 ×0.5	32.00	243★
EMPLOYERS PENSION CONT.	6% × £344	20.64	243★
EMPLOYERS N.I.C.	£344 + £32 = £376 £376 - £84 = £292 £292 × 12.5%	 36.50	 243★

TOTALS FOR POSTING	Code	Amount(£)
	242	344.00
	(W1) 243	89.14

★ Task 2 states that basic pay is coded to labour (third digit 2) and other employee costs (such as overtime premium, employer's pension contribution and employer's NIC) are coded to expenses (third digit 3).

(W1) = £32.00 + £20.64 + £36.50 = £89.14 = £89 (to the nearest £).

ANSWERS (Task 3)

MEMO

To: Liam Green

From: Candy Date

Date: 12 September 2000

Subject: Coding of invoices

Thank you for your note which requested me to check the invoices that you left for me. Please note the following points

- **Invoice from Ince and Sons Brokers**

  This invoice has been coded as an expense for the printing department although it is actually insurance for the whole factory. The total cost of £6,000 should be shared out between all of the departments. Thelma Jones, the management accountant should be able to give you information on the way this cost should be split between the different factory departments.

- **Invoice from Aftercare Limited**

  This invoice is addressed to Cards Delight and not Cards R Us. You should send this invoice on to Cards Delight and also draft a letter to Aftercare Limited explaining what you have done.

- **Invoice from Cellphate Ltd**

  On reviewing this invoice, it does appear to be coded correctly, however, there does appear to be an inconsistency with the goods ordered and the total due. 48 boxes at £25 per box = £1,200 **not** £12,000.

  The purchasing department should be able to advise you of the exact quantity ordered and the price quoted per box of wrapping material. Once you have the relevant information you should contact Cellphate Ltd and ask them to issue a credit note for this invoice and a revised invoice with the correct details and amount due.

ANSWERS (Task 4)

INCOME AND EXPENDITURE BALANCES – Y/E 31/12/2000

Ledger Account	Bal. at 31/7/2000	Amt. coded Aug 2000	Bal. at 31.8.2000
Sales	£	£	£
Birthday Cards			
- U.K.	245,365	38,916	284,281
- Europe	198,467	42,457	240,924
- U.S.A.	231,989	40,061	272,050
- R. of W.	297,946	41,694	339,640
Christmas Cards			
- U.K.	246,578	27,413	273,991
- Europe	316,478	31,076	347,554
- U.S.A.	297,697	34,761	332,458
- R. of W.	399,906	52,316	452,222
Special Cards			
- U.K.	198,464	33,476	231,940
- Europe	201,897	28,094	229,991
- U.S.A.	246,890	40,314	287,204
- R. of W.	299,785	45,761	345,546
Expenditure			
Printing			
- Material	74,789	48,162	122,951
- Labour	61,890	11,467	73,357
- Expenses	93,167	20,439	113,606
Cutting			
- Material	71,789	44,654	116,443
- Labour	58,625	11,461	70,086
- Expenses	75,293	15,064	90,357
Wrapping			
- Material	58,693	8,216	66,909
- Labour	31,704	4,916	36,620
- Expenses	34,471	10,574	45,045
Packing			
- Material	38,568	3,642	42,210
- Labour	36,906	4,508	41,414
- Expenses	48,966	7,784	56,750

ANSWERS (Task 5)

PERFORMANCE REPORT PRODUCTION COST CENTRES TOTAL COSTS – AUGUST 2000				
	MONTH – AUG 2000		YEAR TO DATE	
	Actual £	Budget £	Actual £	Budget £
Material	104,674	108,500	348,513	341,700
Labour	32,352	32,250	221,477	198,500
Expenses	53,861	48,750	305,758	277,100

Workings

	Printing £	Cutting £	Wrapping £	Packing £	Total £
August 2000					
Material	48,162	44,654	8,216	3,642	104,674
Labour	11,467	11,461	4,916	4,508	32,352
Expenses	20,439	15,064	10,574	7,784	53,861
Year to Date					
Material	122,951	116,443	66,909	42,210	348,513
Labour	73,357	70,086	36,620	41,414	221,477
Expenses	113,606	90,357	45,045	56,750	305,758

ANSWERS (Task 6)

DISCREPANCY (VARIANCE) REPORT PRODUCTION COST CENTRES AUGUST 2000		
PERIOD / COST	MONTH £	YEAR TO DATE £
Material	3,826 (F)	6,813 (A)
Labour	102 (A)	22,977 (A)
Expenses	5,111 (A)	28,658 (A)

COMMENT

Significant cost variances more than 10% from budget

- Expenses variance for month of August 2000 = £5,111 (A) = 10.5% (W1)

- Labour variance for year to August 2000 = £22,977 (A) = 11.6%

- Expenses variance for year to August 2000 = £28,658 (A) = 10.3%

$$(W1) = \frac{£5,111}{£48,750} \times 100\% = 10.5\%$$

ANSWERS (Task 7)

SALES PERFORMANCE REPORT – AUGUST 2000				
PERIOD PROFIT CENTRE	MONTH ACTUAL £	MONTH BUDGET £	YEAR TO DATE ACTUAL £	YEAR TO DATE BUDGET £
UNITED KINGDOM	99,805	98,000	790,212	785,000
EUROPE	101,627	109,000	818,469	832,500
U.S.A.	115,136	112,800	891,712	886,400
REST OF WORLD	139,771	142,100	1,137,408	1,164,600

Workings

	Birthday cards	*Christmas cards*	*Special*	*Total*
Month Actual	£	£	£	£
United Kingdom	38,916	27,413	33,476	99,805
Europe	42,457	31,076	28,094	101,627
USA	40,061	34,761	40,314	115,136
Rest of World	41,694	52,316	45,761	139,771
Year to date actual				
United Kingdom	284,281	273,991	231,940	790,212
Europe	240,924	347,554	229,991	818,469
USA	272,050	332,458	287,204	891,712
Rest of World	339,640	452,222	345,546	1,137,408

ANSWERS (Task 8)

NOTEPAD

Key points for telephone conversation with Sales Director

- To show how sales performance is split between the different profit centres.
- To show sales performances for each month and for the year-to-date.
- Comparison of actual performance with budgeted performance.
- Calculation of adverse and favourable variances.
- Managers responsible for the different profit centres should be able to explain any variances which arise.

Lecturers' Resource Pack Activities

CHAPTER 1: INTRODUCTION TO MANAGEMENT INFORMATION

| 1 | **MANAGEMENT REPORT** | Pre-assessment |

What four things might a management information report show?

CHAPTER 2: TYPES OF INCOME AND EXPENDITURE

2   PRODUCTION COST CENTRES   Pre-assessment

How do production cost centres differ from service cost centres?

3   SERVICE COST CENTRES   Pre-assessment

Give three examples of service cost centres.

CHAPTER 3: DOCUMENTATION OF INCOME AND EXPENDITURE

4   DISCOUNTS   **Pre-assessment**

Two types of discount might be offered by suppliers: trade discounts and cash discounts. How do these two discounts differ from each other?

5   ADVICE NOTE   **Pre-assessment**

What information is usually contained within an advice note?

6   DEBIT NOTE   **Pre-assessment**

When might a debit note be issued?

CHAPTER 4: CODING INCOME AND EXPENDITURE

7   CODING ERRORS   Pre-assessment

Why should coding errors be investigated and corrected as soon as possible?

8   SALES ANALYSIS   Pre-assessment

You are checking the standard monthly management report for the sales department which analyses sales by regions: North, Midlands, London and South. It looks like this.

Sales report 30.9.2001

	North		Midlands		London		South	
	Actual	*Budget*	*Actual*	*Budget*	*Actual*	*Budget*	*Actual*	*Budget*
	£'000	£'000	£'000	£'000	£'000	£'000	£'000	£'000
September	30.2	35.0	48.7	50.0	67.1	45.0	21.6	40.0
Year-to-date	297.7	300.0	474.3	470.0	428.9	410.0	412.2	450.0

Do you think any of these figures require further investigation? How would you go about investigating these figures?

BPP
PUBLISHING

CHAPTER 5: REPORTING MANAGEMENT INFORMATION

9   COMMUNICATION METHODS   **Pre-assessment**

What are the four main methods of communication used within an organisation?

10   MEMO HEADING   **Pre-assessment**

What are the four main items of information which should appear at the top of every memo?

BPP
PUBLISHING

CHAPTER 6: MAKING COMPARISONS

11 VARIANCES   Pre-assessment

How are favourable variances different from adverse variances?

12 BONUS   Pre-assessment

A shop owner runs his shop as two different departments which are treated as profit centres: hi-fi equipment and CDs/tapes. Each is run by an assistant earning £1,000 per month plus a half-yearly bonus of 10% of departmental profits after all costs if they meet or exceed planned profit. Planned profit is £3,000 for hi-fi equipment and £4,000 for CDs/tapes. The owner takes £1,500 a month from the business and spends part of her time helping in the shop and the rest on administration/paperwork. The gross profits for the shop for the last six months of trading are shown below. Total shop overheads for the period were £15,648.

	Hi-fi	*CDs/tapes*	*Total*
	£	£	£
Sales	45,280	83,440	128,720
Cost of goods sold	25,232	58,408	83,640
Gross profit	20,048	25,032	45,080

(a) Calculate the bonus for each assistant if all other expenses are shared 50:50 between the departments.

(b) The hi-fi assistant points out that his department only occupies one third of the total shop area but admits that the owner spends 30% of her time in his department and only 20% in the CDs/tapes department. The rest of the time (administration) is applied equally to both departments. Recalculate the bonuses taking these facts into account.

(c) Which calculation do you think the owner should accept?

CHAPTER 7: USING MANAGEMENT INFORMATION FOR DECISION MAKING

13   MARGINAL COSTING   **Pre-assessment**

What is marginal costing?

14   PRICING STRATEGY   **Pre-assessment**

What two basic factors does pricing strategy depend on?

BPP PUBLISHING

Lecturers' practice devolved assessment 1: Panguard Ltd

Performance criteria

The following performance criteria are covered in this practice activity

Element 4.2 Provide comparisons on costs and income

(ii) Information extracted from a particular source is compared with actual results
(iii) Discrepancies are identified
(iv) Comparisons are provided to the appropriate person in the required format

Note: This practice activity asks you to help prepare information for pricing and budgeting and then to compare actual results with the plan, making appropriate comments.

PANGUARD LTD

Panguard Ltd makes high-quality frying pans and has developed a new superior non-stick coating ('Silky') which is to be launched in conjunction with a special five-month sales campaign. The total target sales is 10,000 frying pans. You have been asked to collate some information in order to help with pricing the new frying pans and have received the following estimates from the production department.

	£ per 100 pans
Direct materials	450
Direct labour	200
Factory overheads	350

The marketing department has agreed that £30,000 will be provided for the extra marketing costs required for the sales campaign and the share of other expenses has been set at £25,000 for the campaign period.

Tasks

(a) Calculate the minimum selling price per frying pan if the company policy is to add 25% profit to cost. The minimum price should be rounded up to the nearest £.

(b) The budget for Silky is as follows.

	Month				
	1	*2*	*3*	*4*	*5*
	£'000	£'000	£'000	£'000	£'000
Sales revenue	40	40	40	40	40
Direct materials	9	9	9	9	9
Direct labour	4	4	4	4	4
Factory overheads	7	7	7	7	7
Marketing costs	6	6	6	6	6
Other expenses	5	5	5	5	5
Total costs	31	31	31	31	31

(c)   Actual results (to the nearest £100) are as follows.

'SILKY' CAMPAIGN

	Month				
	1	*2*	*3*	*4*	*5*
Sales in units	1,500	1,800	2,000	2,150	2,300
Sales revenue £'000	30.0	26.0	40.0	43.0	46.0
	£'000	£'000	£'000	£'000	£'000
Direct materials	9.0	8.9	8.9	9.1	9.1
Direct labour	4.0	4.0	4.0	4.0	4.0
Factory overheads	7.0	7.0	7.0	7.1	7.1
Marketing costs	7.0	7.0	6.0	6.0	5.0
Other expenses	5.0	5.0	5.0	5.0	5.0
Total costs	32.0	31.9	30.9	31.2	30.2

Produce a numerical report for management for month 5 and the year-to-date totals showing budgeted and actual costs and revenue and the difference between them (variance). Add a note on the difference between actual and budgeted profit for the period and comment on any trends in the figures which you think are significant.

BPP PUBLISHING

Lecturers' practice devolved assessment 2: Greengrow Ltd

Performance criteria

The following performance criteria are covered in this practice activity

Element 4.1 Code and extract information

(i)   Appropriate cost centres and elements of costs are recognised

(iii)   Income and expenditure are coded correctly

(iv)   Any problems in obtaining the necessary information are referred to the appropriate person

(v)   Errors are identified

Note. This practice activity asks you to code invoices to the correct profit centres, to identify situations when you require further information and how to go about obtaining it. You are also required to spot any errors in items which have already been coded.

GREENGROW LTD

You work for Greengrow Ltd (a garden centre) which sells plants and trees, gardening tools and equipment and also runs a small cafe and gift shop. The accounting system analyses these activities into four different profit centres by using one of the following code prefixes.

P   Plants
T   Tools and equipment
C   Cafe
G   Gifts

The prefix 'O' is used for general overheads and the prefixes are followed by numeric codes to describe the types of revenue or expense involved. Here is an extract from the list of numeric codes.

10   Goods for resale
30   Labour costs
40   Consumable supplies
50   Heat and light
60   Phone and fax
70   Protective clothing
80   Office supplies
90   Miscellaneous

Task

(a)   You are given ten purchase invoices to enter on the system and will need to code them first. Code all that you can and, where you think you do not have enough information to code, explain what you could do to find out the correct code.

1.	£350	Assorted bedding plants
2.	£110	Computer paper and a printer catridge
3.	£150	Working boots and dungarees
4.	£95	Frozen foods
5.	£220	Electricity bill
6.	£1,750	10 lawnmowers
7.	£250	Gardening books and fancy stationery
8.	£300	100 bags of compost
9.	£83	Telephone bill
10.	£36	5,000 carrier bags

Your manager also asks you to check account G10 (Gifts – goods for resale) for last month as the profits 'don't look right'. G10 looks like this.

Date	Invoice	Supplier	Description	£
01.08.2001	148	Jolene	Ceramic pots	450
05.08.2001	375	Smith & Son	Wind chimes	640
08.08.2001	698	Brown Bros	Silk flowers	370
11.08.2001	927	Gomshall Ltd	Garden gnomes	350
14.08.2001	791	Timms Ltd	Border spades	150
19.08.2001	529	Deco Ltd	Birthday cards	95
22.08.2001	847	Tiptoe	Speciality jams	45
25.08.2001	783	Xavier	Feng shui candles	120
29.08.2001	446	Greens plc	Gardening gloves	125

Task

(b)   Which items look as if they might be coded incorrectly? How would you check?

See overleaf for information on other
BPP products and how to order

AAT Order

To BPP Publishing Ltd, Aldine Place, London W12 8AW
Tel: 020 8740 2211. Fax: 020 8740 1184
E-mail: Publishing@bpp.com Web:www.bpp.com

Mr/Mrs/Ms (Full name) _____

Daytime delivery address _____

Postcode _____

Daytime Tel _____

E-mail _____

	5/01 Texts	6/01 Kits	Special offer	5/01 Passcards	Tapes
FOUNDATION (ALL £9.95)					
Unit 1 Recording Income and Receipts	☐	☐			
Unit 2 Making and Recording Payments	☐	☐	All Foundation		
Unit 3 Ledger Balances and Initial Trial Balance	☐	☐	Texts and	£4.95 ☐	£10.00 ☐
Unit 4 Supplying Information for Mgmt Control	☐	☐	Kits		
Unit 20 Working with Information Technology (6/01)	☐	☐	(£80) ☐		
Unit 22/23 Healthy Workplace & Personal Effectiveness	☐				
INTERMEDIATE (ALL £9.95)					
Unit 5 Financial Records and Accounts	☐	☐	All	£4.95 ☐	£10.00 ☐
Unit 6 Cost Information	☐	☐	Inter'te Texts	£4.95 ☐	£10.00 ☐
Unit 7 Reports and Returns	☐	☐	and Kits (£65)		
Unit 21 Using Information Technology	☐		☐		
TECHNICIAN (ALL £9.95)					
Unit 8/9 Core Managing Costs and Allocating Resources	☐	☐	Set of 12	£4.95 ☐	£10.00 ☐
Unit 10 Core Managing Accounting Systems	☐	☐	Technician		
Unit 11 Option Financial Statements (A/c Practice)	☐	☐	Texts/Kits	£4.95 ☐	£10.00 ☐
Unit 12 Option Financial Statements (Central Govnmt)	☐	☐	(Please		
Unit 15 Option Cash Management and Credit Control	☐	☐	specify titles		
Unit 16 Option Evaluating Activities	☐	☐	required)		
Unit 17 Option Implementing Auditing Procedures	☐	☐	(£100)		
Unit 18 Option Business Tax (FA01)(8/01 Text)	☐	☐	☐		
Unit 19 Option Personal Tax (FA 01)(8/01 Text)	☐	☐			
TECHNICIAN 2000 (ALL £9.95)					
Unit 18 Option Business Tax FA00 (8/00 Text & Kit)	☐				
Unit 19 Option Personal Tax FA00 (8/00 Text & Kit)	☐				
SUBTOTAL	£	£	£	£	£

TOTAL FOR PRODUCTS £ _____

POSTAGE & PACKING

Texts/Kits

	First	Each extra
UK (max £10)	£2.00	£2.00
Europe*	£4.00	£2.00
Rest of world	£20.00	£10.00

Passcards/Tapes

	First	Each extra
UK	£2.00	£1.00
Europe*	£2.50	£1.00
Rest of world	£15.00	£8.00

Grand Total (Cheques to *BPP Publishing*) I enclose a cheque for (incl. Postage) £ _____

Or charge to Access/Visa/Switch

Card Number ☐☐☐☐☐☐☐☐☐☐☐☐

Expiry date _____ Start Date _____

Issue Number (Switch Only) _____

Signature _____

We aim to deliver to all UK addresses inside 5 working days; a signature will be required. Orders to all EU addresses should be delivered within 6 working days. All other orders to overseas addresses should be delivered within 8 working days. * Europe includes the Republic of Ireland and the Channel Islands.

REVIEW FORM & FREE PRIZE DRAW

All original review forms from the entire BPP range, completed with genuine comments, will be entered into one of two draws on 31 January 2002 and 31 July 2002. The names on the first four forms picked out on each occasion will be sent a cheque for £50.

Name: _____   Address: _____

_____

_____

How have you used this Devolved Assessment Kit?
(Tick one box only)

☐ Home study (book only)
☐ On a course: college _____
☐ With 'correspondence' package
☐ Other _____

Why did you decide to purchase this Devolved Assessment Kit? *(Tick one box only)*

☐ Have used BPP Texts in the past
☐ Recommendation by friend/colleague
☐ Recommendation by a lecturer at college
☐ Saw advertising
☐ Other _____

During the past six months do you recall seeing/receiving any of the following?
(Tick as many boxes as are relevant)

☐ Our advertisement in *Accounting Technician* magazine
☐ Our advertisement in *Pass*
☐ Our brochure with a letter through the post

Which (if any) aspects of our advertising do you find useful?
(Tick as many boxes as are relevant)

☐ Prices and publication dates of new editions
☐ Information on Interactive Text content
☐ Facility to order books off-the-page
☐ None of the above

Have you used the companion Interactive Text for this subject?   ☐ Yes   ☐ No

Your ratings, comments and suggestions would be appreciated on the following areas

	Very useful	Useful	Not useful
Introductory section (How to use this Devolved Assessment Kit etc)	☐	☐	☐
Practice activities	☐	☐	☐
Practice devolved assessments	☐	☐	☐
Trial run devolved assessments	☐	☐	☐
AAT Sample simulation	☐	☐	☐
Lecturers' Resource Pack activities	☐	☐	☐
Content of answers	☐	☐	☐
Layout of pages	☐	☐	☐
Structure of book and ease of use	☐	☐	☐

	Excellent	Good	Adequate	Poor
Overall opinion of this Kit	☐	☐	☐	☐

Do you intend to continue using BPP Assessment Kits/Interactive Texts/? ☐ Yes ☐ No

Please note any further comments and suggestions/errors on the reverse of this page.

Please return to: Nick Weller, BPP Publishing Ltd, FREEPOST, London, W12 8BR

REVIEW FORM & FREE PRIZE DRAW (continued)

Please note any further comments and suggestions/errors below

FREE PRIZE DRAW RULES

1   Closing date for 31 January 2002 draw is 31 December 2001. Closing date for 31 July 2002 draw is 30 June 2002.

2   Restricted to entries with UK and Eire addresses only. BPP employees, their families and business associates are excluded.

3   No purchase necessary. Entry forms are available upon request from BPP Publishing. No more than one entry per title, per person. Draw restricted to persons aged 16 and over.

4   Winners will be notified by post and receive their cheques not later than 6 weeks after the relevant draw date.

5   The decision of the promoter in all matters is final and binding. No correspondence will be entered into.